# TV and Cars

*To Jo*

# TV and Cars

Paul Grainge

EDINBURGH
University Press

Edinburgh University Press is one of the leading university presses in the UK. We publish academic books and journals in our selected subject areas across the humanities and social sciences, combining cutting-edge scholarship with high editorial and production values to produce academic works of lasting importance. For more information visit our website: edinburghuniversitypress.com

© Paul Grainge, 2022

Edinburgh University Press Ltd
The Tun – Holyrood Road
12(2f) Jackson's Entry
Edinburgh EH8 8PJ

Typeset in 12 on 14pt Arno Pro and Myriad Pro
by Cheshire Typesetting Ltd, Cuddington, Cheshire

A CIP record for this book is available from the British Library

ISBN 978 1 4744 8003 1 (hardback)
ISBN 978 1 4744 8004 8 (paperback)
ISBN 978 1 4744 8005 5 (webready PDF)
ISBN 978 1 4744 8006 2 (epub)

The right of Paul Grainge to be identified as the author of this work has been asserted in accordance with the Copyright, Designs and Patents Act 1988, and the Copyright and Related Rights Regulations 2003 (SI No. 2498).

# Contents

List of Figures vi
Acknowledgements vii

Introduction: Vehicles for Television 1

1. The Trip 20
   On journeys and passengering

2. Carpool Karaoke 52
   On the drive to platforms

3. Peter Kay's Car Share 84
   On commuting and commonplace roads

Conclusion: Mobility and Media 117

Notes 127
Bibliography 135
Index 144

# Figures

| | | |
|---|---|---|
| 1.1 | Framed inside the car, *Marion and Geoff* (2000) | 23 |
| 1.2 | Cars in vistas, *The Trip to Spain* (2017) | 32 |
| 1.3 | The SUV as celebrity 'auto-du-jour', *The Trip to Spain* (2017) | 34 |
| 1.4 | The female space of cars, *Better Things* (2016) | 37 |
| 1.5 | Dynamics of passengering, *The Trip to Italy* (2014) | 42 |
| 2.1 | Feeling the car, *Comedians in Cars Getting Coffee* (2019) | 61 |
| 2.2 | 'I just called to say James loves you', Stevie Wonder in 'Carpool Karaoke' (2015) | 68 |
| 2.3 | Vlogging in vehicles, *Dad V Girls* (2018), from the *Dad V Girls* YouTube channel https://www.youtube.com/watch?v=xgy_WHe_NRs (last accessed 12 July 2021) | 72 |
| 2.4 | In the grounds of the White House, Michelle Obama in 'Carpool Karaoke' (2016) | 78 |
| 3.1 | John's Fiat and the anthropology of the road, *Car Share* (2015) | 92 |
| 3.2 | The incredulity of drivers, *Car Share* (2017) | 95 |
| 3.3 | Daydreaming during the commute, 'Rush Hour' in *Car Share* (2017) | 101 |
| 3.4 | The exuberance of singing in cars, *Car Share* (2017) | 103 |
| 3.5 | Glancing at Forever FM, *Car Share* (2015) | 104 |

# Acknowledgements

The seed of this book began through an accidental conversation with Karen Lury and I am grateful to Karen and Amy Holdsworth as series editors, and Gillian Leslie at Edinburgh University Press, for driving things forward.

The project took shape at the end of a four-year secondment to the Midlands4Cities Doctoral Training Partnership and I would like to thank the 'dream team' of Susanna Ison, Sam Offiler, Claire Thompson and Leslie Bode for providing support and humour as mutual passengers on the M4C journey. I also appreciate the patience and good grace of my colleagues in the Department of Cultural, Media and Visual Studies at the University of Nottingham who might have been forgiven for wondering if I was ever returning.

I wrote this book during the coronavirus pandemic in 2020 and early 2021. I was extremely fortunate, in a very difficult time, to have the space to think about the experience of 'being together' in cars when social distancing was the norm and people spent time indoors, not on roads. My Dad and my sister Cath have been a constant source of chat and cheer even though visits to Pompey were curtailed for a year. My sons, Daniel and Joseph, were remarkable during the various waves of lockdown and home-schooling and I thank them for creating and sharing all the small pleasures, even when these involved outright mockery of me. I have been sustained and inspired by my children throughout.

Finally, I owe more than I can say to Jo Gregory, whose capacity for kindness, cocktails and puns has no limit. From the first time she parked 'Dora the Explorer' outside my house, I have thanked my lucky stars.

# Introduction:
# Vehicles for Television

For many children who grew up in the UK during the 1980s, the Saturday television schedule offered a bonanza of cars. The weekend offered reruns of *Bonanza* (NBC, 1959–73), too, but that was another vehicle entirely. I have never been a car fanatic or someone who likes the sound of engines or burning rubber enough to be called a 'petrol-head'. My interest in TV shows that discuss the finer points of Ferrari is fleeting at best. However, as a child in the early eighties who liked to play with Matchbox cars – die-cast toys owned by most boys in my school – I knew the weekend would provide a spectacle of automobiles.

This was true across a range of TV genres. Friday evenings on BBC1 would see *Starsky and Hutch* (ABC, 1975–79), the American crime show about two streetwise detectives who drove an iconic Ford Gran Torino, nicknamed the 'striped tomato' for its bright red colour and distinctive white vectors.[1] Saturday would produce a parade of vehicles in various states of gleam, motion, dirt and disrepair. Dominating Saturday afternoons on BBC1 was *Grandstand* (BBC1, 1958–2007), a three-hour sports programme covering favourites such as football but also including minority sports that the BBC helped develop for television, like Rallycross. Early evening provided the highlight of the schedule, BBC1 offering *The Dukes of Hazzard* (CBS, 1979–85), which guaranteed a car chase in 'The General Lee', and ITV showing *Knight Rider* (NBC, 1982–86), the crime-fighting series featuring David Hasselhoff and a talking Pontiac Trans Am called KITT. Saturday viewing would finish with a gameshow like *The Price is Right* (ITV,

1984–88), classic light entertainment where excitable contestants would 'Come on Down' to up the prize stakes from cheeseboards and dishwashers to caravans and cars, all swooningly displayed by models in evening wear.

There are many ways to consider the relationship between television and cars. Automobiles have long been a fixture on TV screens and provide a way to think about multiple facets of television production, history, genre, aesthetics, distribution, formats, fandom, as well as popular memory. While the title *TV and Cars* may create expectations about the kind of programme this book is about, cars lift the bonnet on the study of television in more ways than one. Whenever a contestant would squander the chance of winning the car on the darts-based gameshow *Bullseye* (ITV, 1981–95) – another staple of my TV weekend in the 1980s – the host Jim Bowen used a refrain that rubbed salt in the proverbial wound: 'look at what you could have won'. There is a similar element of consolation in this book for those anticipating a chassis-loving, engine-roaring, tyre-squealing treatment of automobiles on screen. My primary concern is not with programmes about cars, per se, but the way that television comedy represents the social life of cars: how people talk, feel, think, sing, dream and behave in the habitat of a car and through the act of 'passengering'. Before explaining this, it is useful to consider some alternative ways that a volume on TV and cars could be approached. For motor enthusiasts and fans of Jeremy Clarkson, consider this a moment where I wheel in vehicles, three in this case, and say 'look at what you could have read'.

Cars help tell histories of television production and programming. Rallycross on *Grandstand* is 'Vehicle 1', an indicative racing example that can be used to unpack the long history of sports broadcasting in a particular national context. The popularity of motorsport on British television, and around the world, is generally associated with Formula 1 grand prix racing, combing its heady mix of superstar drivers and commercial sponsorship. As a global phenomenon, motorsport is estimated to sustain a combined television audience of one billion people and generate a £50 billion annual industry turnover (Haynes and Robeers 2020: 410). The history of televised motorsport does not begin with Formula 1, however. In the British context, there was a formative period in the 1950s and 1960s when the BBC cultivated 'tailored-for-television' motor racing events, from hill climbs (uphill trials driving) to Rallycross (combining track and off-road racing). These events were enabled by developments in outdoor broadcasting but also shaped by industrial factors such as the launch of ITV in 1955, a new commercial channel which led the BBC to extend coverage of sport to broaden its appeal with audiences.

Richard Haynes and Timothy Robeers explain that the early difficulty of motorsport for television production 'was transforming the spatial dimensions of sporting action for the small screen, thereby making the action intelligible for the audience' (Ibid.: 416). Developing motorsport for television brought into view aesthetic considerations, specifically how to keep fast-moving cars in focus on long tracks with bends, curves and other visual obstructions. Haynes and Robeers argue that motorsport was actively created and represented in the post-war period as a competitive and dramatic spectacle *for television*. With Formula 1 becoming a global media franchise, the impetus for dramatic TV spectacle has continued apace. Fitting mounted onboard cameras to all F1 cars, which became the norm in 1998, is one device of many used to enhance track-level excitement. From Rallycross and Formula 1 to American stock car racing (NASCAR) and endurance events such as Le Mans, the coverage of motorsport invites multiple perspectives on television's industrial and aesthetic history.

Cars can also tell stories of genres and formats. 'Vehicle 2' is what some claim to be the most watched television show in the world, *Top Gear*, viewed by 500 million people in 117 countries according to some estimates (Bonner 2010). As a child in the 1980s, I had no interest in the original *Top Gear* (BBC2, 1977–2001) with its earnest mix of car reviews, road safety and consumer advice. However, the series was relaunched in 2002, retooled from a car magazine show to a lifestyle entertainment vehicle (BBC2/BBC1, 2002–present). This transformation illuminates key developments in the business of television, signalling both the rise of lifestyle programming in the late 1990s and the onset of what Jean K. Chalaby (2016) calls 'the format age'.

The UK version of *Top Gear* is broadcast internationally. The show's makeover in 2002 focused on the personalities and foibles of three middle-aged male presenters and emphasised set-ups and stunts, mostly involving driving expensive cars or transforming old cars into something else, such as amphibious vehicles, and then racing them. This formula made stars of the presenters (Jeremy Clarkson, Richard Hammond and James May) as well as the anonymous silent racing driver 'The Stig'. However, *Top Gear* is also a format and exemplifies the rise of format trading in the global TV marketplace. Rights to the show have been licensed around the world and local versions of *Top Gear* have been made in countries ranging from France and Italy to Russia, China and the United States. The commercial value of the show was such that *Top Gear* became the first original programme to be ascribed the status of 'BBC Worldwide Global Brand'. After Clarkson's acrimonious split with the BBC in 2015, a take on the format with the same three presenters was made for Amazon Prime Video.[2] This was called *The Grand Tour* (2016–present) to avoid any legal dispute over the words 'top' or 'gear'. Proving the popularity of hedonistic masculine motoring shows, Clarkson's presenter-led mix of motoring challenges, timed laps, studio segments and celebrity guests was equally successful on streamed TV.

Frances Bonner asks why, given *Top Gear*'s phenomenal success, the show has not been considered more by academics in Television Studies. She posits various possible reasons, including the 'cheerfulness with which it espouses its unfashionable positions on cars, masculinity and the environment' (Bonner 2010: 43). However, the contrarian politics of *Top Gear* are not the only reason for the programme's relative 'invisibility' in media analysis; Bonner points to the continuing relegation of popular television more broadly among TV scholars. Cars not only tell stories of genres and formats, in this respect, but also help demonstrate which genres, and types of TV, have been privileged within academic study. Together with mainstream programmes like *Top Gear*, niche channels are populated with shows dedicated to car restorations, stunts, auctions and other motoring hobbies and fascinations. These often come with memorable titles such as *Chop Cut Rebuild* (Speed, 2004–13), *Mud, Sweat and Gears* (BBC America, 2015–present), *Lost in Transmission* (History, 2015) and *Bangers and Cash* (Yesterday, 2019–present). In favouring genres like news and drama, Television Studies has often overlooked daytime staples, of which there are many car varieties. Critical focus has also tended to steer away from docusoaps like *Traffic Cops* (BBC1/BBC3/Channel 5, 2003–present) among other auto-focused shows that are popular mainstream fare but low in prestige.

The relation between TV and cars is not restricted to the programmes that make up the television schedule. Automobiles are also a distinctive feature of the commercials, promos and sponsorship messages that surround TV shows. Cars are routinely encountered in the 'interstitial' moments of television, the bits in-between the programmes. Enter 'Vehicle 3' in its covetous spectacle. Of all television forms, spot commercials have experimented most consistently with camerawork, lighting, sound, special effects and story to envision automobiles on TV screens. One of the most successful print and TV ad campaigns of the last century was introduced in 1959 for Volkswagen. Regarded as a harbinger of 'creative advertising', VW's campaign for the Beetle asked audiences to 'think small', turning the traditional value of car size on its axles. Memorable slogans remain key within television advertising, giving rise to commercials that depict vehicular prowess and the pleasure of driving in tones that veer between broodingly atmospheric and cloyingly chirpy – from 'Vorsprung durch Technik' (Audi) to 'Zoom-Zoom' (Mazda).

Although television advertising is often explicitly gendered, it has not circumscribed the role of women, and the image of female drivers, as predictably as TV motoring shows which remain stubbornly attached to male-bonding rituals. Car ads are crucial to the economics of the commercial television industry. At the same time, they point to the popular imagination of automobiles in media representation, including recurrent themes of power, control, individuality and freedom. In the UK, where my own nostalgia pools, young adulthood in the 1990s was accompanied by a popular series of television commercials for the Renault Clio. Playing on ideas of French style and refinement, these ads involved the tantalisingly chic 'Nicole' confidently driving her car to meet boyfriends beyond the watchful gaze of 'Papa'. The auto-centric story of 'Nicole' and 'Papa' would demonstrate the capacity of advertising to become entertainment in its own right, a decade before 'branded content' took hold within marketing parlance (Grainge and Johnson 2015: 23–53). The campaign lasted seven years and culminated in a marriage spoof based on *The Graduate* (1967), 'Nicole's' unlikely betrothal to (what was revealed as) the comedian Vic Reeves ending in her equally unlikely elopement with Vic's sidekick Bob Mortimer. After years of female independence driving her Renault, it was indicative that 'Nicole's' new husband took the wheel of the Clio in the last scene, but the ad brought a clever denouement to a popular car-based serial.

Cars are prolific within television advertising and feature prominently in the commercials and sponsorships that interrupt, anticipate and punctuate TV programmes. Automobiles also appear in paratextual forms such as titles and trailers, especially when cars assume a narrative or character status in a show. In a colourful animated example, the title sequence of the Hanna-Barbera series *Wacky Races* (CBS, 1968–69) would delight in parading a crazy grid of roadsters, buzz wagons, chuggerbugs and converter-cars. In the high concept style of American TV in the 1980s, the title sequence of *Knight Rider* would dwell more on the sleek lines and pulsating red bonnet of KITT, a computationally pimped sports car driving across sand flats at dusk. Prefiguring the software aesthetic of twenty-first-century car design, KITT became the literal vehicle for 'a shadowy flight into the dangerous world of a man who does not exist'. In the world of TV promos, trailers have made frequent use of automobiles. In forty seconds or less, cars can underline both the genre and conceit of a programme. To take one example, the BBC trailer for *Life on Mars* (BBC1, 2006-7) – a police procedural about a detective from 2006 who suddenly wakes up in 1973 – dramatised the backwards leap in time by having the protagonist's BMW transmute into a Ford Cortina, the UK's most popular car in the seventies. The entire concept of the show was captured through the sight of a gear stick turning, magically, from ergonomic steel grey to retro wooden brown.

It has become de rigueur in TV drama for police detectives to drive an automobile that personifies them, from Starsky's 'striped tomato' and the vintage Jaguar synonymous with *Inspector Morse* (ITV, 1987-2000) to Saga Norén's 'hunter green' Porsche in *The Bridge* (DR1, 2011-18). As Jonathan Bignell (2016) notes, cars often have a life of their own within the fictional world of the television police series. However, cars can assume character status in comedy, too, both in ambient ways and more directly. The iconic yellow New York cab established the premise of the popular American sitcom *Taxi* (ABC, 1978-82, NBC, 1982-83). Set in a New York fleet garage, the atmospheric title sequence focused on a cab driving across the Queensboro Bridge into Manhattan, the distinctive colour and chequered badge of the taxi becoming part of the promotional image of the show. Sometimes, the personality of a car can become a marketing synecdoche. When the popular British sitcom *Only Fools and Horses* (BBC1, 1981-2003) was brought back to screens in 2001 after a five-year break, the trailer used a single, twenty-second, visual gag. Drawing on Del Boy's dream (turned reality) of becoming a millionaire, the promo transformed the show's most famous prop – a decrepit yellow three-wheeler van – into a stretch version of itself, parked outside a casino in Monte Carlo (Bryant and Mawer 2016: 149-50). The incongruous sight of a Reliant Regal turned into a limousine with 'New York·Paris·Peckham' painted on the side became an immediate way to announce the new prosperity of Britain's most famous market trader.

Cars are part of television's nostalgic iconography and have become artefacts of TV merchandise. My own toy collection in the 1980s included Corgi models of the red Ford Gran Torino from *Starsky and Hutch* and the white Jaguar XJS from *Return of the Saint* (ITV, 1978–79).[3] My children have also owned a host of TV-based toy cars, often based on British children's programmes like *Roary the Racing Car* (Channel 5, 2007–10) that were quick to capitalise on the popularity of animated automobiles in the late 2000s, turbo-charged by the Pixar franchise *Cars* (2006). Playing on the material culture of television memory, entire museum collections have been built on the promise of visitors seeing vehicles from television up close. Between 1989 and 2011, the 'Cars of the Stars Motor Museum', improbably situated in the Lake District in the UK, housed vehicles ranging from Del Boy's Reliant Regal and KITT from *Knight Rider* to Mr Bean's Austin Mini and the two remaining GMC vans from *The A-Team* (NBC, 1983–87).[4] Cars are props but can also become enduring TV personalities, physical vestiges of a programme's afterlife (Holdsworth 2011).

Motorsport, lifestyle formats and advertising and promotion provide three different angles on the relationship between television and cars. In each case, the televisual focal point is the automobile itself. Cars are a defining feature of modern culture and it should be no surprise that television, the defining mass medium of the twentieth century, has been drawn to the life, look and pursuits of automobiles. However, cars are more than the sum of their spoilers and cylinders. They are also spaces, habitats and dwelling places; their confined interiors are sites of talk, living and feeling among drivers and passengers. Lucy Fife Donaldson and James Walters (2018) provide a different way of looking at television and cars in this context, concentrating on the vehicle as an environment for TV performance. Rather than examine programmes *about* cars, they explore the multitude of ways that cars feature in 'linking moments' in TV dramas, focusing on instances where cars transport characters from A to B as opposed to becoming a pretext for a stunt, chase or handbrake turn. They examine sequences that are not about the vehicle in action but that use the restricted space of the car to draw out expressive details of character interaction and social behaviour.

The title sequence of *The Sopranos* (HBO, 1999–2007) provides a contrast to the titles of *Knight Rider* in this respect. As Donaldson and Walters note, cars have been used in TV drama as 'a space that expresses a character's relation to their wider world' (Ibid.: 360). This is signalled from the outset in *The Sopranos* by a brooding title sequence that charts Tony Soprano's (James Gandolfini) commute from New York City to his suburban New Jersey home. The interior of the car becomes an intimate frame for the character of Soprano, a mafia boss in control of his world but often pensive and prone to panic attacks. The title sequence concentrates on the driver's view of passing signposts, turnpikes, toll booths, telephone wires, billboards and traffic, which are intercut with close-up interior shots of Tony smoking a cigar, gripping the steering wheel and eventually parking in his drive, climbing out of the vehicle and shutting the car door. The tone of the sequence is one of strength in repose. However, Donaldson and Walters explore how the safe space of the car also becomes dangerous and claustrophobic for Soprano in the series, the first episode of Season 2 showing Tony slumped at the wheel after an anxiety attack brought on by his unbridled rage at the car's faulty CD player. Whether inviting pleasure or anger, calm or incredulity, automobiles can provide a space to unwind, daydream or actively let rip. These feelings play out on roads which have their own rules, rhythms and social anthropology. Describing the activity of driving and the comportment of drivers, Joe Moran observes that motorists 'behave like a micro-society, without ever imagining themselves as one' (2009: 8).

Exploring the wide range of feelings that cars elicit, Mimi Sheller suggests that 'movement and being moved together produce the feelings of being in the car, for the car and with the car' (2004: 222). She uses the term 'automotive emotions' to help think about felt relationships between car, self, family and friends. These affective and sensory energies are often dramatised in TV, expressed in representational tropes where cars become a setting for emotions on a spectrum ranging from kinship and affinity to loneliness and solitude. The poignancy of the stationary vehicle, parked to allow the occupant a moment of life reflection, is one of many examples. An iconic TV commercial for Nescafé in 1988 called 'Sunrise' illustrates this trope, depicting a melancholy woman who parks her VW Beetle on a clifftop looking out to sea. As the ad unfolds, the car shifts from a lonely to a restorative scene, the woman preparing a coffee inside the vehicle and getting out to sit on the bonnet, warming her body and spirits at the 'fresh start' of the beautiful sunrise. The Jimmy Cliff song 'I Can See Clearly Now' underscores the connection between car, coffee and self in this moment of renewal. Automobiles are not simply a functional or masculine space; they embody feelings and dispositions among car users that are as significant to understand in TV representation as the spectacular display of horsepower or gadgetry.

Sheller writes of the 'emotional geographies of the car', delineating scales that range from the 'individual body within the car, to the familial and sociable setting of car use, to the regional and national car cultures that form around particular systems of automobility' (Ibid.: 236). Sheller's use of the term 'automobility' taps into sociological discussion about 'car culture' and 'driving culture' that emerged in the 2000s as part of wider debate about the significance of movement and mobility in social life. This discussion incorporates infrastructural issues and spatial histories around transportation systems, roadways, city layouts and suburban development, as well as regulatory concerns with congestion, pollution, speed, safety and road deaths. However, the concept of automobility also encompasses in-car behaviours, cultural uses, sensory pleasures and driving dispositions. In her book *In the Company of Cars*, Sarah Redshaw puts forward a series of questions that explore driving as a social and cultural practice. Reflecting on a highly familiar experience, these questions likely chime with anyone who has taken the wheel of a car:

> Who do we become when we get into a car and take to the roads? Are we different people when we are behind the wheel, protected by the metal shell that enables us to insert ourselves into public domains from the comfort of

> our very own living room on wheels? What expectations do we have as drivers and how does the traffic and road system measure up to those expectations? How do we relate to the regulation of our driving by authorities and what ambiguities exist in our relationship to cars? What does being a driver demand of us? (2008: 1–2)

Although car cultures vary in different national contexts, and can be experienced unevenly within those contexts, automobiles structure the way that many people live and work, travel and commute. Automobiles have levelled a huge impact on communities and the way we live, for better and for worse. They inscribe a sense of freedom of movement while continuing to pollute the environment through carbon emissions; they offer travel and flexibility but can become a bullying presence for pedestrians and within transport policy; they invite people to define themselves socially and individually but often in ways that are stratified by age, socio-economic background and assumptions around gender. Automobility denotes a complex network and infrastructural system but also an intricate part of our personal and collective life (Featherstone 2004).

It is not my intention in this book to examine the sociology of driving culture but I do want to think about the social dimension of mobility that attends to *being in cars*, and how this has been represented on TV. The area of social theory that bears most directly on my concerns in this context is the 'sociology of passengering'. This concept has been developed extensively by two scholars in the field of human geography, Eric Laurier and Hayden Lorimer, who have undertaken ethnographic study of the car as 'habitat'. The purpose of their research, which I discuss in Chapter 1, is to bring to light some of the 'subtle problems and possibilities of travelling together' in vehicles (Laurier, Lorimer et al. 2008; Laurier and Lorimer 2012). Drawing on video records of ordinary car travel, Laurier and Lorimer analyse what people do in cars and how they do it. Specifically, they focus on forms of conversation that occur during car journeys and how talk and social interaction are organised in the small space of car interiors.

The visually framed, front-facing nature of car passengering makes it highly suited to the 'small screen aesthetics' of television (Creeber 2013). This is especially so in contemporary situation comedy where scenes of domesticity, a staple of traditional sitcom, have been creatively displaced to the 'comfort of our very own living room on wheels'. Developments in mobile camera technology since the 2000s have made cars a more prevalent setting for television genres that might once have relied on studio-based filming. Comedy entertainment is notable in this regard. Reflecting on the number of shows based on conversation between two people in the front seat of a car – from Jerry Seinfeld's *Comedians in Cars Getting Coffee* (Crackle/Netflix, 2012–17, 2017–20) to *Peter Kay's Car Share* (BBC1, 2015–18) – the columnist Stuart Heritage observed in 2018 that 'the car-cam' has become comedy's favourite vehicle (Heritage 2018). From sitcoms and chat shows to comedy drama and digital shorts, the interior space of the car has become a more regular scene for television 'two-handers', entertainment focusing on talk and interaction between a driver and passenger.

In terms of production, the availability of high-quality miniature cameras, typified by GoPro devices, has enabled greater mobility and cost-effectiveness filming inside cars. Jonathan Bignell (2016) notes that the significance of cars on television is dependent on an industrial history in which changing production circumstances affect how cars appear on screen. He suggests that cars have been represented differently in TV programmes depending on what can be achieved with available cameras and technologies of sound recording. These production circumstances often shape aesthetic styles and filming conventions. While a variety of camera angles are commonly used in TV shows to shoot the interior of cars – the front windshield, the close-up passenger point-of-view, from the back seat or from the side or rear-view mirror – certain screen genres have been shaped by the aesthetic of the dashcam. In the last two decades, a number of factual entertainment and online video formats have used dashcams to mediate the 'private' space of the car. From TV docusoaps like *Britain's Worst*

*Driver* (Channel 5, 2002–3) that deployed dashboard cameras to film the agonies of hapless drivers, to newer forms of social media entertainment where YouTube creators vlog inside vehicles to address online communities up close, cars have become a scene of small screen intimacy.

The purpose of this book is to 'think through' developments in contemporary television while also thinking through critical discussion about the social life of cars. In taking an auto-centric approach to TV, I focus on contemporary comedy entertainment and the particular conceit, and treatment, of passengering. It is of course possible to explore the social life of cars through numerous television genres, from drama and documentary to factual entertainment, lifestyle shows and TV road trips of various kinds.[5] However, I would argue that comedy is an especially rich site for exploring dynamics of passengering in an increasingly mobile media environment. In a culture where media is more transportable, and screen content can be produced and consumed on the move, car-based comedy drove into view in the 2010s. Whether long journeys, short drives or everyday commutes, passengering became a deliberate premise in various popular entertainment vehicles, a trend that can be seen to speak, in different ways, to transitions in UK and US television culture.

The three main examples of this book – *The Trip*, 'Carpool Karaoke'[6] and *Peter Kay's Car Share* – all centre on relations and behaviours in the habitat of a car. They connect in this way to other comedy examples that use automobiles and passengering as an explicit proposition (*Marion and Geoff, Carpool, Comedians in Cars Getting Coffee,* the vlog series *Dad V Girls*) or that use the social life of cars to advance character relations through driving scenes (*Gavin and Stacey, Better Things, Curb Your Enthusiasm, I'm Alan Partridge, The Big Bang Theory,* amongst others).[7] Concentrating on car-based comedy may at first seem niche, but I would argue that taking a thematic approach to a particular TV situation can provide a prism on television as a small screen medium. The focus on cars does not simply invite textual analysis in this context. Although each chapter of this book proceeds with a principal programme or 'text' in view, my examples invite different ways of looking at television. In critical terms, the theme of cars allows manoeuvring between methodological and disciplinary lanes rather than occupying a single track within TV studies.

For instance, my auto-centric examples enable perspectives on media industry development. To varying degrees, *The Trip*, 'Carpool Karaoke' and *Peter Kay's Car Share* all became test balloons of the 'distribution revolution' transforming the film and television industry in the 2010s (Curtin, Holt and Sanson 2014). *The Trip* series was distributed at international film festivals as well as on public service and pay TV, 'Carpool Karaoke' exemplified the porous borders of television and YouTube, and *Peter Kay's Car Share* was the first original BBC1 content to launch on the Corporation's streaming service, iPlayer, before broadcast transmission. Each programme (or unbundled segment of a network show in the case of 'Carpool Karaoke') assumed something of a hybrid identity in form and distribution. While targeting different audiences, and using alternative means, they demonstrate how comedy became a conduit for the permeability of TV entertainment in the 'post-network' era.

At the same time, car-based comedy invites thinking about genre and aesthetics. This book ranges across several media genres – sitcom, talk show, web series, social media vlogging – and does not proclaim to be a study of any one genre specifically. Neither is it about TV comedy in a strict historical or theoretical sense (see for example Kamm and Neumann 2015; Marx 2019; Mills 2009). Rather, my examples highlight how established and emerging genres, aligned with comedy entertainment, have sought to respond to changes brought about by a pervasive sense of mobility within everyday media life. Ethan Tussey (2018) suggests that the era of smartphones, tablets and internet-connected mobile devices has thrown into relief moments and spaces where people consume media between work and leisure. These transitory moments include daily routines such as the commute, which often take place in cars. Tussey demonstrates how the mainstreaming of mobile technology led many companies in the

2010s to consider the social dimensions of public space within media use; he examines how the entertainment industry developed products, apps and services for 'mobile parts of the day'. However, these 'in-between' moments also gave creative impetus to TV and digital comedy. As a small screen conceit, the social life of cars became a subject of popular entertainment in the 2010s, a media expression of a more general sense, and aesthetic, of mobility within audiovisual culture.⁸

Extending from questions of aesthetics, one can draw out specific points about cultural representation. The use of cars in television comedy is nothing new. Automobiles have been deployed in various ways and for different purposes, from the wailing siren in the parodic title sequence of *Police Squad!* (ABC, 1982) to the car capers in the physical comedy of *Mr Bean* (ITV, 1990–95). A short-lived American sitcom in the 1960s, *My Mother the Car* (NBC, 1965–66), was even based on the fantasy of a man whose deceased mother is reincarnated as an antique car and who communicates with her son through the car radio.⁹ Throughout the history of TV comedy, automobiles have been used for throwaway gags, slapstick sketches and fantasy rides. The examples in this book, however, depict the social life of cars through conventions of realism. As naturalistic representations of driving and passengering, explicitly focused on social practices inside vehicles, my case studies invite thinking about the role that TV comedy plays in the formation and reflection of values and identities around automobility.

Juergen Kamm and Birgit Neumann observe that 'concepts of class, gender, ethnicity, disability, sex, family, work and domesticity find a most intriguing and provocative expression in TV comedies' (2015: 1). Within this intersectional mix, gender remains a prevailing concept in the arrangements of driving and passengering in TV comedy. In each of my case studies, men drive, women are passengers, and the habitat of the car is shaped by the driver as 'host'. Although examples of comedy drama like *Better Things* (FX, 2016–present) depict the car as a female space and move beyond representations that are focused simply on shopping runs or chauffeuring children, automobiles are a space where talk and togetherness have their own everyday politics. *TV and Cars* is decidedly *not* about men and their machines. However, men tend to occupy the driving seat in TV comedy, literally and figuratively, and this gendered pattern is a subtext in the dynamics of passengering in the 2010s that I explore.

The three main examples in *TV and Cars* fall between 2010 and 2020. This may feel suspiciously neat but there are reasons to identify the 2010s as a significant cultural moment in the broader history of television. Examining the transformation of TV in this decade, brought about by changes in how television was developed, distributed, quantified, curated, regulated, experienced and understood, M. J. Robinson talks about 'all-encompassing disruptions' to the medium (2017: 10). More directly, Catherine Johnson links transition to the impact of the internet on the delivery of television. She writes, 'what changed around 2010 was the increased ubiquity of the internet as a means of delivering television programming and other audiovisual content to audiences, facilitated by the rise of superfast broadband and 4G, adoption of tablets and smartphones, and increased ownership of internet-connected television sets' (2019: 3). The launch of Apple's iPad in 2010 would in many ways herald the culture of mobile TV viewing. The proliferation of portable screen devices went hand-in-hand with the burgeoning influence of internet-delivered television, from the growth of video-on-demand services like Netflix to the ubiquity of open platforms such as YouTube. Television was shaped by an emerging portal logic in the 2010s and Chapter 2, specifically, provides a way to consider these developments through TV-digital hybrids like 'Carpool Karaoke'.

Despite the rise of streaming platforms and online delivery in the 2010s, Derek Johnson (2018) reminds us that portal logics have not obliterated the significance of television channels. The case of *The Trip* and *Peter Kay's Car Share* demonstrate the resilience of traditional broadcasting even as programmes, channels and media companies have experimented with new strategies of TV circulation and release. In the UK context, *The Trip* and *Peter*

*Kay's Car Share* throw into relief a TV landscape shaped by the enduring presence of the BBC. While *The Trip* went on a content journey of its own – travelling from the BBC to Sky and released as a boutique film franchise in the US – *Peter Kay's Car Share* became a means of representing ordinary British life on roads and then, unexpectedly, *remembering* that life as part of the BBC's public service response to the coronavirus pandemic. Pursuing its mission to 'inform, educate and entertain', the BBC made the sitcom available as a 'box-set' on its iPlayer service during lockdown in 2020, five years after the show's release. In the midst of rupture caused by Covid-19, the social proximity of passengering became suddenly comforting and nostalgic. While the period of this book considers a particular juncture in the contemporary history of television, marked by the growing articulation of mobility and media, it is also bracketed by a cataclysm in 2020 that brought a pause in people's relation with movement, commuting, cars and the road.

As a means of focus, *TV and Cars* draws on British and American examples and in so doing connects television with the culture of automobility in specific national contexts. Although the genesis of 'Carpool Karaoke' was British and led to subsequent TV versions in Italy and the United Arab Emirates, it was a product of Hollywood and would reflect rituals of carpooling in the US, notably Los Angeles. Meanwhile, *The Trip* and *Peter Kay's Car Share* were creations of the British TV industry and would tap into car-based rituals, scenes and mentalities of UK driving culture. There are no doubt other ways of examining car-based comedy that reflect different national television markets and experiences of the road. It is perhaps indicative that the *Worst Driver* format has been developed in versions around the world, with series in Brazil, Canada, Poland and New Zealand to name just four. The US and UK do not have a monopoly on car-based television, and the rambunctious driving cultures of nations like Italy or India provide rich material for comedy entertainment, inviting localised versions such as *Carpool Karaoke Italia* (Italia1, 2017) but also other ways of drawing humour from the motorscapes, manoeuvres, forms of car etiquette and gestures of road annoyance considered normal in national settings (Edensor 2004: 112).

My intention in this book is to use each chapter as a dual carriageway in critical terms: primarily to use car-based comedy to engage with debates about contemporary television in Anglo-American contexts, but also to consider the way that television helps think about the sociology of passengering. I draw on various literatures in doing so and switch between lanes at times, but my hope is to create insights across different fields, and keep things moving, rather than cause the analytic equivalent of a pile-up. Each chapter combines a particular type of comedy entertainment with a specific mode, and representation, of automobility. Chapter 1 explores *The Trip* series as a hybrid 'comedy of distinction' (Mills 2009: 134), a programme where automotive and gastronomic journeys become a context for ruminations on middle-age, masculinity, celebrity selfhood and the contemplative nature of being together in cars. Chapter 2 examines 'Carpool Karaoke' as a primary expression of the 'drive-and-talk' in the 2010s, a nascent micro-genre straddling television and digital media that literally performs the act of singing in the private space of automobiles. Chapter 3 uses *Peter Kay's Car Share* to analyse constructions of the ordinary in television sitcom, the show's depiction of commuting capturing the mundane anthropology of the road and the affinities that people find through everyday chat, gossip, music and daydreaming inside of vehicles. The conclusion parks the discussion by reflecting on the critical gains of bringing media studies and mobility studies together.

As may be clear from this introduction, a hazard of writing a book called *TV and Cars* is the pull of vehicular metaphors. There is broader history here. Automotive metaphors have emerged in historical moments to conceptualise film, television and media at large, from the language of 'star vehicles' coined in Hollywood's studio era to the way the internet was described as an 'information superhighway' for much of the 1990s. Cars are woven into metaphors that we use to make sense of the world, including our media world. I make no apology for drawing on images of traffic, motoring, roadmaps and so forth, but simply warn of metaphors ahead. When I was a child, my parents would sometimes give me and my sister an I-Spy book that challenged us to spot things from the car to pass time on the annual journey to a holiday caravan park. These spotters' guides (now owned by the tyre company Michelin) were a treat for the road. While there are no points for spotting vehicular metaphors in this book, you might consider their fleeting appearance as I-Spy for the read. Whether or not you are familiar with the programmes I discuss in this book – and you don't need to be – my hope is that, cumulatively, they provide a way of comprehending tendencies in contemporary television while offering a screen view of our cultural relationship with cars. With that, I suggest that we get things into gear.

# 1
# The Trip
## On journeys and passengering

In 1997, UK television audiences were introduced to Maureen Rees, a Welsh cleaner who became the star of a BBC docusoap called *Driving School* (BBC1, 1997). Following a group of learner drivers attempting to pass their driving test, *Driving School* was part of the boom in popular factual entertainment in the 1990s. One of a number of TV shows taking a documentary approach to everyday subjects, Maureen became a household name for her wincing lack of driving ability. Watched by 12 million viewers, *Driving School* was an early form of reality television, blending fly-on-the-bonnet filming with the soap opera storyline 'will Maureen ever pass?' Narrated by Quentin Wilson, the original co-host of *Top Gear* and subsequent creator of *Britain's Worst Driver*, *Driving School* would frequently veer into situation comedy. This was notable in scenes where Maureen's car would hit curbs and drift into fast lanes and a dashboard camera would provide reaction shots of Maureen's husband, Dave, sitting terrified in the passenger seat. Affectionately dubbed 'the driver from L', Maureen briefly became a national celebrity, releasing a cover version of the Madness song 'Driving in My Car' and fronting a government campaign to increase road awareness. In style and content, *Driving School* made clear the television mileage to be gained from filming inside cars, including the social relationships of driving and passengering that occur in the front seats.

Three years after Maureen and Dave became fixtures of British television, BBC2 would broadcast a mockumentary about a different couple, *Marion and Geoff* (BBC2, 2000–3). Experimental in form, this innovative comedy series assumed the style of a video diary and was filmed entirely within the confines of a car. The series featured a naively enthusiastic taxi driver called Keith Barret (played by Rob Brydon) coming to terms with separation from his wife Marion and his two young children, or 'little smashers'. The first series comprised ten episodes, nine minutes in length, each presented as a monologue to a camera mounted on Keith's dashboard. As a study in comedy pathos, Keith's optimistic faith in other people belies his own isolation as he drives from London to Cardiff in failed attempts to see his children, parking wistfully outside the home of Marion and her new lover Geoff. The series is sparse in the way that it uses the vehicle as a space, situation and narrative frame. Brett Mills coins the term 'comedy verité' to describe a naturalist tendency in sitcom during the 2000s. Such programming, he writes, 'resolutely rejects the theatrical nature of sitcom, abandoning the laugh track and offering a visual style which positions the viewer as an observer of everyday behaviour' (2009: 128). Referring to *Marion and Geoff* as an early example, Mills suggests that the camera functions as a confessional in the series, the humour lying in 'the gap between the truth which Keith attempts to construct (and clearly believes) and that which is apparent to everyone else' (2004: 75).

Within the hybrid documentary modes of *Driving School* and *Marion and Geoff* the car becomes a 'habitat', in the sense of being a home or environment. Within social science research, the idea of the car as 'habitable' space has been used to understand how vehicles become a setting for family, friendship, acquaintances, emotional crisis, talk, singing, anger and all manner of other behaviours. An ethnographic research project called 'Habitable Cars', carried out in the late 2000s, used in-car video footage to examine the interactions between people during day-trips, school drop-offs, commutes and shopping runs (Laurier, Lorimer, Brown et al, 2008). Using digital camcorders to record journeys as they happen – in different cars, in various social configurations, doing alternative activities – the project analysed the complex relations and exchanges that take place in cars. The interior of any vehicle will of course vary depending on size, model and brand. However, all cars are confined; their arrangement of side-by-side and row-by-row seating produces proximity, and invites intimacy, of a certain kind. Mimi Sheller talks about the 'lived experience of dwelling with cars' (2004: 222). The language of dwelling reinforces the automobile as a mobile space that we *inhabit*, a domestic environment on wheels.

Television has long been drawn to depictions of the domestic, especially in situation comedy where the family and the home become ways of representing everyday life. In different respects, *Driving School* and *Marion and Geoff* translate domesticity to the car; they establish characters, environments and plots that recur within the front seat of a small vehicle. The car is not a prop in either context but a key part of each programme's identity. Establishing the car as a space of small screen intimacy, they both demonstrate the way that cameras have been used inside vehicles and beyond television genres that focus simply on motoring or sport.

Sarah Cardwell (2015) uses *Marion and Geoff* to think about the role of TV aspect ratios in framing television space. In a period in the early 2000s when the 'cinematic' potential of television was prominent within industry and marketing talk, *Marion and Geoff* was unusual for its 'stripped down' look and 'muted mise-en-scène' (Peacock 2006: 116).[1] Filmed exclusively in medium close-up using a 4:3 aspect ratio, Keith's head and upper body are framed in the square confines of his driving space.

Cardwell argues that 'the particular achievements of Series 1 of *Marion and Geoff* are its bold restrictions of visual space and its focus on Keith's monologue, and the way in which it creates a visible frame-within-a-frame to create an oppressive sense of his being precisely *separated* from the outside world' (2015: 93). This 'frame-within-a-frame' is achieved by keeping events within the vehicle; the restrictions of space heighten a sense of intimacy with Keith, a man whose solitary life is played out in his car, on roads, and through hapless attempts to converse with toll booth attendants. In a resonant scene, Keith reflects positively on his relation-

Figure 1.1 Framed inside the car, *Marion and Geoff* (2000)

ship with the man with whom his wife has eloped, saying 'I would never have met Geoff if Marion hadn't left me, not a chance of it. We're in different worlds. He's in pharmaceuticals; I'm in cars – literally – *I'm in the car*'.

Keith Barret became a breakout role for Rob Brydon and marked the start of Brydon's highly successful career in television and film, specifically in UK comedy and light entertainment. This would include a longstanding collaboration with Steve Coogan, whose company Baby Cow Productions made *Marion and Geoff*. If we are to trace the development of contemporary car-based comedy in the UK, Rob Brydon and Baby Cow Productions provide a significant thread. Not least, they connect *Marion and Geoff*, *Gavin and Stacey* (BBC3/BBC1, 2007–10, 2019) and *The Trip* (BBC2/Sky Atlantic/Sky1, 2010–20), three acclaimed UK sitcoms based, with different premises, on the representation of cars, roads, people and journeys. Brydon has been literally 'in the car' as naïve Keith Barret, as a version of himself in *The Trip*, and as Uncle Bryn in *Gavin and Stacey*, a comedy which makes a deliberate theme of car journeys between England and

Wales. Meanwhile, Coogan's enduring comic persona of Alan Partridge has been associated with motoring ever since *I'm Alan Partridge* (BBC2, 1997–2002), a sitcom which saw the inept but narcissistic broadcaster move semi-permanently into a roadside 'Travel Tavern'. As one of the writing team on the series, Armando Iannucci notes that *I'm Alan Partridge* used the sitcom as 'a kind of social X-ray of male middle-aged Middle England' (Husband 2019). Cars became, and remain, a mark of Alan's self-image in this context; Partridge is a driver who wears tan leather driving gloves, scrupulously observes the Highway Code, categorically refuses to downsize his Rover 800 to a mini metro and adopts a motoring worldview influenced by the reactionary blokey-ness of *Top Gear*.

Coogan has frequently placed Alan Partridge at the wheel of a car. In the film based on the TV character, the opening sequence of *Alan Partridge: Alpha Pappa* (2013) provides an extended sequence of Alan driving a saloon around the Norwich ring-road, singing Roachford's 'Cuddly Toy' with naff swagger while also managing to inform a passing driver that their 'fog lamps are on'. The importance of cars to the Partridge character was such that Coogan avoided a driving ban in 2019 after arguing that a ban would jeopardise the livelihood of crew members contracted to a new TV series featuring Partridge in a motor travelogue. Coogan said in court, 'The whole nature of the series is that it is a travelogue and it's an artistic thing that he drives and that defines his character. You couldn't put him on a train because that is not who he is – it's part of his character that he drives' (Waterson 2019). In the case of Alan Partridge, cars and the comportment of the driver provide comedic grist to a popular television character. A more sustained and deliberate use of the car can be found in *The Trip*, a collaboration over four series (set in England, Italy, Spain and Greece) between Coogan, Brydon and the film and television director Michael Winterbottom.

Car journeys are a recurring motif in *The Trip* series and provide signposts for this chapter and the book as a whole. In opening out questions about contemporary television, *The Trip* illuminates the production and distribution of TV comedy, the generic and aesthetic hybridity of sitcom, and the representation of cars as a space of interaction (in this case between two male celebrities). However, *The Trip* is also a representation of automobility. In particular, the series provides a vehicle for conceiving the car as habitat and as a way of being together. The dynamic of 'passengering' underpins this book, and I seek to establish the concept in this chapter by examining the types of talk and togetherness that occur between middle-aged men in the midst of hiatus.

## Navigating *The Trip* as television

*The Trip* includes four discrete six-part series that were broadcast in the UK, and distributed internationally, between 2010 and 2020. In each series, Steve Coogan and Rob Brydon play fictionalised versions of themselves on restaurant assignments for *The Observer*, a Sunday broadsheet newspaper. Driving to fabulous restaurants in beautiful corners of Europe, the two men eat food across tables while competing in words, wits, quips, sniping, career reflection, life rumination and general comic one-upmanship. The latter is channelled through a relentless stream of celebrity impressions. Having established early careers as voice artists (Brydon known for his mellifluous advertising voice-overs and Coogan for doing character voices on the satirical puppet show *Spitting Image* (ITV, 1984–1996)), impressions recur in each series and veer freely from Michael Caine to Mick Jagger, Anthony Hopkins to Al Pacino, Richard Burton to Ronnie Corbett.

All four series involve an epicurean tour of fine eateries, loosely tied to a literary touchstone. *The Trip* (BBC2, 2010) sees 'Coogan' and 'Brydon'[2] driving between high-end restaurants and gastro-pubs in the Lake District and Yorkshire Dales, the landscape of northern England providing opportunities to riff and reflect on the literary sites of Wordsworth and Coleridge. *The Trip to Italy* (BBC2, 2014) becomes an explicit pilgrimage to Byron and Shelley, the chosen restaurants situated in locales where the Romantic poets lived, from Liguria and Rome to Amalfi and Capri. *The Trip to Spain* (Sky Atlantic, 2017) moves from Cantabria in the north of Spain to Andalusia in the south, the duo literally dressing up as Don Quixote and Sancho Panza for an *Observer* photo-shoot in one episode. Finally, *The Trip to Greece* (Sky1, 2020) recreates Odysseus's journey home from Troy, tracing a path in restaurants from Turkey to Ithaca, via Lesbos, Pilos, Athens and Hydra. Despite the literary allusions, the premise of each series amounts to two middle-aged men driving in cars, eating in restaurants and doing celebrity impressions. Coogan summarised the formula by saying, 'we drive through the most spellbinding scenery that I've ever seen in my life, and then we diminish it by talking crap' (Jones 2014).

The programme became an unlikely hit and had its own distribution journey in the 2010s, broadcast as four self-standing TV series but also re-cut as feature-length movies shown at the Toronto International Film Festival (*The Trip*), Sundance Film Festival (*The Trip to Italy*) and Tribeca Film Festival (*The Trip to Spain*). While *The Trip* was positioned as arthouse film in North America – *The Atlantic* describing it as a 'curious little franchise' and 'the perfect piece of British comedy comfort food' (Sims 2017) – the series was made for television first and foremost.[3] Jointly developed by the production companies co-owned by Coogan (Baby Cow Productions), Rob Brydon (Arbie and later Small Man Productions) and Michael Winterbottom (Revolution Films), *The Trip* was initially broadcast on BBC2. This was in-keeping with BBC2's reputation for niche and eclectic programming. According to Simon Winchester, former Creative Director of the channel, 'BBC1 is like a supermarket, BBC2 more like a deli' (cited in Brownrigg and Meech 2011: 74). *The Trip* served up a mélange within the terms of this metaphor. In blending genres, the series was described variously as an 'unstructured, unscripted circumnavigation of a comedy show' (Barton 2014) and a 'classy mash-up of *Top Gear*, *MasterChef* and *Curb Your Enthusiasm*' (Hogan 2017b).

The genesis of *The Trip* sprang from the on-screen double act of Coogan and Brydon in Michael Winterbottom's film *A Cock and Bull Story* (2005). This playful meta-comedy saw the pair play themselves on the set of a movie adapting Laurence Sterne's eighteenth-century novel *Tristram Shandy*. The film includes in-the-wings conversations between the duo that often lampoon Coogan's status-anxiety as star. This theme would be reprised in *The Trip*, a semi-improvised comedy where the protagonists present sauced versions of themselves, 'Brydon' the affable family man and staple of British light entertainment and 'Coogan' the award-winning but self-regarding comedian-cum-actor with tangled personal life. In choosing television for their subsequent collaboration, Winterbottom explained:

> the thing with comedy, especially film comedy, is the more plot you put into it, the less funny it is. There's always this tension between the bits that are story and the bits that are funny. With a sitcom, you accept that there isn't a plot … We have the advantage of there being no story. Nothing happens, so it's easier to be funny'. (cited in Newbould 2017)

The BBC's former Head of Comedy Entertainment, Jon Plowman, likewise points to the difference between film comedy and TV sitcom, reflecting: 'a sitcom can just "be", but a film has to have a *story*, a structure, something that keeps an audience in their seats and is worth 90 minutes of their time' (2018: 280). On these terms, 'story' in sitcom is less important than episodes that return to established characters, settings and behaviours.[4] Accordingly, *The Trip* series returns to the performance of two known comedians eating in restaurants, driving in cars, occasionally phoning agents, personal assistants and partners, and engaging in competitive improvisation. *The Trip* was nominated in 2011 for the BAFTA television award for Best Situation Comedy and Coogan won the award for Best Male Comedy Performance in the same year. Brydon was later nominated for the same category in 2018 for his role in *The Trip to Spain*.

British television comedy has been funded, in the main, by the BBC and Channel 4 as public service broadcasters. Coogan and Brydon have both established careers as national comedy mainstays in this milieu. However, the history of *The Trip* is linked to the growth of the independent production sector at the turn of the millennium. Following regulatory shifts designed to stimulate competition in the UK television marketplace, production companies like Baby Cow flourished in the 1990s and 2000s, to the extent that 77 per cent of BBC comedy commissions were being won by the independent sector in 2010, the year *The Trip* first aired (Mills and Horton 2016: 34).[5] Although BBC Worldwide (the commercial arm of the Corporation) bought a quarter stake in Baby Cow Productions in 2008, *The Trip* defected from the BBC to the satellite provider Sky for its third series. This would demonstrate the growing clout of comedy departments in the world of pay TV, but also the challenge the BBC faced, and continues to face, holding onto signature programmes against well-financed commercial rivals.[6]

Signalling Sky's investment in 'top-flight original comedy' (Sherwin 2016), *The Trip to Spain* was promoted as a prestige show and released on the premium channel Sky Atlantic alongside a roster of high-end dramas such as *Game of Thrones* (HBO 2011–19), *Big Little Lies* (HBO, 2017–19) and *Fortitude* (Sky Atlantic 2015–18). According to Sky at the time, 'comedy is having a renaissance across the key broadcasters so we are entering a noisy room and we need to get noticed' (cited in Mills and Horton 2016: 39). Poaching *The Trip to Spain* from the BBC was part of Sky's strategy of 'making noise' in this context. Releasing the series on Sky Atlantic gave the show immediate stature, an acquisition placed in the company of flagship programmes aired by Sky Atlantic as the 'home of HBO' in the UK. While *The Trip to Greece* would move to Sky1 when released three years later, the sheen of Sky Atlantic gave the acquisition of *The Trip* the promotional veneer of 'quality TV'.

*The Trip* is a niche comedy series and selecting it for analysis might be seen as another example of academic writing choosing to focus on a programme with 'cultural capital': a show that does something different for a discerning audience as opposed to a more 'ordinary' and broadly popular sitcom. However, part of the interest of *The Trip* is the show's awareness of its own discerning status. To utilise another useful term by Brett Mills, it is a 'comedy of distinction', referring to sitcoms 'which offer audiences the pleasures of *not* being traditional, and engage in industrial and textual work in order to distinguish themselves from traditional sitcom as far as possible' (Ibid.: 134).

Reviewing *The Trip* as a festival film, *Daily Variety* characterised the release as a 'two-hander road movie', applauding its mix of virtuoso impressions and gastronomic voyeurism as 'comedy for smart people' (2010). In the show's concern with themes of ageing, Steve Coogan described it as '*Last of the Summer Wine* for *Guardian* readers' (Ellis-Petersen 2017). Both comments acknowledge the programme's address to middle-class taste. The fictional premise of the series is explicitly linked to the lifestyle sections of a broadsheet newspaper, and *The Trip* exploits and satirises the taste formations of weekend magazine supplements, targeted as they are to 'defined levels of taste, experience, education, income and aspiration to match advertising demographics' (Morris 2015: 440). However, the series also gestures to lifestyle television formats as part of its 'industrial and textual work', mingling the sensuous presentation of food served up by *MasterChef* (BBC1/BBC2, 1990–2001, 2005–present) with road adventures in gleaming automobiles reminiscent of *Top Gear*.[7]

The description of *The Trip* as a 'road movie' by the Hollywood trade publication *Daily Variety* points to the way that cars are central to the programme's identity. Deborah Allison (2013) notes that the road movie is a genre to which Michael Winterbottom has often returned. Winterbottom began in television, making TV dramas and documentaries for Thames Television in the late 1980s and early 1990s. Collaborating with the screenwriter Frank Cottrell Boyce, Winterbottom's film debut was *Butterfly Kiss* (1995), a work intended for broadcast on the BBC but which won accolades on the international film festival circuit. Winterbottom has moved freely between television and film during his career, developing a reputation for experimenting with genres including the road movie, war films, science fiction, docudrama, westerns and biopics. *Butterfly Kiss* was Winterbottom's first outing on the road.[8] Far from the glorious sojourns of *The Trip*, there is a desperation to the road in *Butterfly Kiss*; the film depicts a female serial killer prowling motorway service stations in Lancashire with a naïve young girl as accomplice. Accordingly, there is a sense of transience in the places (service stations, motels) and people (hitchhikers, truck drivers, travelling salesman) that the protagonists encounter. Thematically, the film plays with the road movie's preponderance for representing disenfranchised individuals going on journeys of self – trips that are psychological as much as geographical (Allison 2013: 2–3).

*The Trip* is a world away from the bleak landscapes and liminality of *Butterfly Kiss*. However, there are characteristics in Winterbottom's style that endure. Allison notes that most of Winterbottom's films 'show a dedication to a mediated realism'. She writes, 'from the outset, his work has been characterised by a strong commitment to location shooting. Over time, his use of improvisation and non-professional actors has increased, as has his use of handheld camerawork and natural lighting to capture the spontaneity of performance and their real world backdrops' (Ibid.: 190). These traits of location shooting, script improvisation, agile camerawork and real settings are demonstrated in the four outings of *The Trip*. This is experienced, pointedly, in the use and depiction of cars. In the next section, I consider different ways that automobiles inform the visual, thematic and representational identity of the series.

## Automobile aesthetics, celebrity selfhood and SUVs

Shortly after *The Trip to Spain* launched on Sky Atlantic, Volvo began a promotional campaign to sponsor the channel, broadcasting fifteen-second sponsor messages that depicted separate panoramic scenes: one of children running to the sea from a Volvo parked on a beach and another of two Volvos driving along a clifftop, coastline in view. Each carried the message 'Watch the full film: search *The Unseen Ocean*'. Prefacing programme title sequences, these sponsor messages – what TV promotion specialists call 'bumpers' – functioned as trailers for an online video series about the use of cars by 'defiant pioneers'.[9] Claiming Volvo's green credentials, *The Unseen Ocean* served to communicate a message about environmental sustainability. In doing so, the promos used aerial perspectives of cars travelling through landscape, a form of auto spectacle that would also be displayed in *The Trip* series.

Aerial shots of cars are common in TV representation. Panoramic views of vehicles often feature in spot commercials, channel sponsorships, title sequences and TV shows, a style of image that resonates across television's flow of ads, paratexts and programmes. The representation of cars on TV has developed a visual grammar that frequently involves shifts in camera perspective. The title sequence of the Danish crime series *The Bridge* (DR1, 2011–18) is replete with these shifts and exemplifies the way that aerial views of cars are routinely intercut with road-level perspectives. The titles comprise a montage of vehicles driving across the bridge that links Malmö and Copenhagen. Seen at night from high above, the slow movement of car lights is intercut with close-ups of rain beads on the bonnet of Saga Norén's signature Porsche. Michael Winterbottom uses similar intercuts, pointing to the way that scale is used to develop narrative, define space and create mood through the image of vehicles. It is perhaps fitting in *The Trip* that 'Coogan' and 'Brydon' drive a Range Rover as the auto-maker's airy brand slogan 'above and beyond' aptly describes Winterbottom's use of cameras at different range: aerial shots, close-ups from behind the back seat, medium long-shots from the car travelling in front. Mediated realism is not simply a case of placing cameras inside cars. In each series of *The Trip*, interior shots of the vehicle are interposed with aerial views of

Figure 1.2 Cars in vistas, *The Trip to Spain* (2017)

automobility, creating shifts in perspective that veer between proximity and vistas.

In a bonus feature on the DVD of *The Trip*, Coogan remarks, 'I feel like I'm in an advert for a Range Rover'. The parallel is instructive as *The Trip* series is, at times, reminiscent of advertising in both the style of filming and the echo of actual TV ads. In one episode of *The Trip to Spain* ('La Posada del Laurel'), a driving scene shows 'Brydon' and 'Coogan' break into a rendition of 'The Impossible Dream', the popular song from the 1965 musical *Man of La Mancha*. The song refers to the 'quest' of Don Quixote, a playful intertext in the series. While the reference is ostensibly musical and literary, the famous Andy Williams version of the song was also used in a lavish TV commercial by Honda in 2005 to accompany its brand slogan 'the power of dreams'. In both *The Trip* and the Honda commercial, images of vehicles are used in spellbinding scenery to accompany the 'questing' driver.[10] By Helen Wheatley's definition of 'spectacular television', *The Trip* delivers visual pleasure by representing cars in ways that are 'designed to be stared at, to be ogled, contemplated and scrutinised, to be gaped and gawked at' (2016: 1). Exploiting new capacities of high-definition (HD) filming and drone-based camerawork, these pleasures become more pronounced in each series. From snaking switchbacks in Liguria to the parched valleys and ravines of Rioja, panoramic views are taken to new and literal heights in Italy, Spain and Greece.

*The Trip* involves fluid movements between sweeping exterior shots of the car and confined, interior space where the two men talk and jest. These transitions create a distinct yoking of journey and joking within each series. In a programme where comedy actors bicker over impressions of David Bowie and Alan Bennett, and the gameshow *Bullseye* is referenced as readily as Fellini's *La Dolce Vita* (1960), one might ask what, or who, the joke is on? The answer, most immediately, is 'Coogan' and 'Brydon'. According to Michael Allen and Janet McCabe, the series constructs 'a parodic slippage between the already-known male performers and the fictionalised versions of those selves' (2012: 151). In the first episode of *The Trip to Italy* ('Il Cenobia dei Dogi'), 'Brydon' reflects that he is 'not as affable as his public persona' while 'Coogan' is jokingly summarised as 'pompous, aggrandising, self-conceited and up his own arse'. Performing scripted roles, but with high degrees of improvisation, *The Trip* series plays with 'possible but unverifiable glimmers of truth' in the portrayal of comedy and celebrity self (Morris 2015: 435). This includes the relation and expression of self through cars.

*The Trip* follows other self-referential sitcoms in this respect, notably *Curb Your Enthusiasm* (HBO, 2000–present), where Larry David performs a misanthropic version of himself. Cars are often used in television sitcoms to project the personality traits of characters. In *Curb Your Enthusiasm*, the hybrid Toyota Prius helps connote the character of Larry as a smug Hollywood liberal ('we're Prius drivers, we're a special breed' he snaps in one episode when snubbed by a fellow owner).[11] By contrast, 'Coogan's' choice of a Range Rover in *The Trip* is a signifier of celebrity, the high-end sports utility vehicle (SUV) having become, since the 2000s, an 'auto-du-jour' of the rich and famous. As a projection of character, the selection of a Range Rover enables *The Trip* series to play with Coogan's real-life reputation as a motor enthusiast

Figure 1.3  The SUV as celebrity 'auto-du-jour', *The Trip to Spain* (2017)

while parodying 'Coogan's' semi-fictionalised relation with celebrity culture and its trappings.

Coogan's interest in cars is largely known through tabloid reporting of his extensive automobile collection and driving bans, and through his appearances on *Top Gear* in the 2000s.[12] Cars have been a theme in press interviews throughout Coogan's career. In publicity for *The Trip to Greece*, Brydon goaded his co-star about his material wealth during an interview with *The Guardian Magazine*, mischievously saying in front of the reporter, 'tell her about your cars'. Coogan replied dryly:

> Cars are weird because cars are a way of me disengaging from anything creative or ethical – it's like a brain holiday. I don't actually drive them all. I use public transport a lot . . . But I collect them. Some people meditate. I can't do that. So I source old cars and restore them. (Barton 2020: 20)

The opposition that Coogan sets up between automobiles and 'anything creative or ethical' is revealing, echoing liberal sleights of value around car ownership that are picked up in *The Trip* series.

In the first series of *The Trip* ('The Inn at Whitewell'), for instance, 'Brydon' remarks to 'Coogan', 'I wouldn't have had you down as having a four-wheel drive'. Deflecting that the Range

Rover was his girlfriend's idea ('Coogan's' planned passenger before she flew back to New York) the comment is open-ended. In *The Trip to Greece* ('Troy to Kavala'), 'Brydon' is more explicit in drawing attention to Coogan's run of cars, telling a jobbing actor and musician volunteering at the Moria refugee camp in Lesbos how many cars his friend owns (nine). Driving to the camp, 'Coogan' acts on the defensive, explaining that the Range Rover is loaned to him and is, nevertheless, 'a hybrid, half electric, so it kind of cushions the impact that a monster gas guzzler normally has'. The visual contrast between the gleaming car and the barbed wire camp, and 'Coogan's' half-hearted claims about the green credentials of the 4x4, are part of the political undercurrent that distinguishes much of Michael Winterbottom's work.

While the politics of *The Trip* are lightly drawn – restaurant scenes linger on sweating kitchen workers as well as sumptuous Michelin dining – the series is attuned to the ironies of automobility. This includes the 'greenwashing' that car brands like Land Rover (among others) pursue in promoting their commitment to the environment, a rhetorical strategy that often masks complicity in the environmental crisis (Miller 2017). Between 2010 and 2018, SUVs doubled their global market share from 17 to 39 per cent, putting them ahead of heavy industry, aviation and shipping in terms of global carbon emissions (Kommenda 2019). Accounting for 700 megatonnes of $CO_2$ a year (more than the yearly total emissions of the UK and the Netherlands combined), rhetoric about the hybrid credentials of SUVs are little more than a promotional gesture, a drop in the unseen ocean. *The Trip* is alert to the impact of SUVs but unable to resist the cachet of driving the 'monster gas guzzlers' in question.

Examining the growing popularity of SUVs among suburban mothers at the turn of the millennium, Sarah Lochlann Jain suggests that SUVs have been marketed as a vehicle that 'can uniquely fuse the hitherto "uncool" aspects of family life with the hipness of the outdoor adventure' (2002: 398). In her argument, the 'masculine' appeal of the SUV merges with gendered practices of mobility and motherhood where SUVs are linked to 'an understanding of "safety" that relies on chauffeuring children as much as "winning" in potential car accidents' (Ibid.: 398). In parallel, she suggests that SUVs enable 'men's idealization of the car as a means of escape and a tool for identity', striking in the way that high-tech 4×4s are frequently advertised as a way of getting closer to nature. SUVs present an interesting point of comparison in the use and gendering of vehicles in TV comedy. They feature differently, for example, in *The Trip* and the American comedy drama *Better Things*, a series that is similarly concerned with a middle-aged voice artist and acting professional working in the entertainment industry, Hollywood in this case.

*Better Things* came to prominence in 2016 as a semi-autobiographical series starring and co-written by Pamela Adlon. Different from *The Trip*, but contemporaneous to it, Adlon plays a divorced single mother, Sam, raising three daughters and managing her family, friendships, work and sex life amidst the emotional and physical transitions of being in her late forties and early fifties. Like many TV series set in Los Angeles, cars become part of the narrative fabric and weave themselves into the show's bittersweet storylines. Focusing on what Alexandra Schwartz (2020) terms the 'functionally dysfunctional matriarchy' of Sam, her kooky mother and three daughters, the show plays out a number of key moments, conversations and interactions in Sam's SUV, many of which involve 'chauffeuring children'. While *Better Things* does not restrict the representation of vehicles to parenting – in Season 4, Sam replaces her 'Mom-mobile' for a two-seater El Camino with the refrain 'welcome to my midlife crisis' – the series depicts the gendered space of the car in a different way to *The Trip* series.

The final episode of the first season ('Only Women Bleed'), for example, is punctuated by three extended scenes inside Sam's family-sized Chrysler. Before the title sequence, we see Sam lugging suitcases into the back of the car, followed by a shot of Sam and her mother talking in the front seats, the viewer looking as if riding in the rear. After shutting the trunk and pulling off the drive, Sam stops the car and slumps on the steering wheel, realising that she doesn't have the emotional reserve to take her eccen-

**Figure 1.4** The female space of cars, *Better Things* (2016)

tric mother on their planned trip. In the second car scene, Sam is crawling in LA traffic, having dutiful phone-sex with her lover while distractedly hunting for a water bottle, the viewer watching as if in the passenger seat. As the car and her lover inch forward, she takes a more urgent call from her middle daughter's school, typical of the way that *Better Things* depicts Sam constantly juggling her personal and parenting life. In the very last scene, providing the emotional culmination of the first season, Sam and her daughters drive along a highway, listening to Alice Cooper's 'Only Women Bleed'. In this moment, the car becomes a space of family connection. Shot from different perspectives in and around the car, the scene shows each daughter singing reflectively, the eldest daughter feeling the air outside the car and Sam reaching back to touch her youngest daughter's hand. The series ends with a mid-range shot of the car travelling towards the camera with a dedication from Paula Adlon as showrunner, writer, producer and star, 'to my daughters'.

The 'habitat' of the car is figured differently in *The Trip* and *Better Things*. Both series reflect poignantly on family, friendship, parenting and ageing, but the car, and more precisely the SUV, is a different site of 'dwelling' in each case. In one, it is an extended space for family and personal relationships and in the other it is a rented space of male escape. Neither comedy is about the car per se but automobiles are rarely incidental; they provide a conduit for key moments of dramatic and comedic interaction. Lucy Fife

Donaldson and James Walters argue that car interiors often transcend their 'functional status as a means of moving characters between more discernibly climactic locations', providing a performance environment for representing inter-personal relations in nuanced and meaningful ways (2018: 356). Cars are constrained spaces but can provide opportunities for 'expressive rapport' between actors and characters, an issue I return to in Chapter 3.

The Trip does not fetishize automobiles but is aware of their signifying presence, both in cultural terms and as a foil for jokes about film and television. In *The Trip to Italy*, 'Coogan' suspects that 'Brydon' has booked a Mini Cooper (the only time they depart from a Range Rover) just so that he can do impressions of Michael Caine from *The Italian Job* (1969). Referencing contemporary TV trends, a restaurant scene in *The Trip to Spain* ('La Posada del Laurel') has 'Brydon' tell 'Coogan' that he has just received a text 'from James [Corden] travelling to work... on Sunset Boulevard'. Pricking 'Coogan's' professional sensitivity to rivals who have 'made it' in America (ergo James Corden, Ricky Gervais, Simon Pegg, Sacha Baron Cohen), 'Brydon' taunts him, 'the big thing is Carpool Karaoke... two men singing in cars'. The reference is deliberate as the pair intersperse their own front-seat conversations with occasional moments of singing: 'The Impossible Dream' while driving through Spain, The Bee Gees' 'Tragedy' in Greece and a full catalogue of songs by Alanis Morissette in Italy.

Music is used in the series to establish mood. In the very first episode of *The Trip*, 'Coogan' puts on Joy Division's brooding song 'Atmosphere' as they drive through the ruddy pastoral landscape of the Yorkshire Dales. 'Why are we listening to this?' asks 'Brydon', perplexed, to which 'Coogan' pretentiously replies, 'That's what I've chosen as the soundtrack for this landscape'. The song accompanies picturesque shots of the Range Rover snaking along rural B-roads, the car partly obscured by dry stone walls as it glides through rolling scenery in long autumnal shadows. The choice of Joy Division is knowing on several levels. Not only is Coogan from the North West, but he also played Tony Wilson in Michael Winterbottom's *24 Hour Party People* (2002), a film about the record label that launched Joy Division. More broadly, however, the song cues the melancholy tone of *The Trip* as a series. This is accentuated by Michael Nyman's piano solos that instil a sense of mournfulness at the end of each episode.

Examining the first series of *The Trip*, Michael Allen and Janet McCabe suggest, 'the question that hovers across the six episodes is: what if the best is already behind you before you have even had a chance to realise personal ambitions and your true worth?' (2012: 155). Each series of *The Trip* involves constant bickering and comparing of how the two men's careers are progressing, from 'Coogan's' desire for greater Hollywood recognition to 'Brydon's' ventures into film acting. Wives, girlfriends and children are acknowledged but exist in the background. This adds poignancy to meditations on male middle-age across *The Trip*, from laments on the passing of female interest (all the while flirting and sleeping with several women during their trips) to choices made about the balancing of career and family responsibility. The latter is reinforced by a contrast between 'Brydon's' affectionate phone calls home to his wife and 'Coogan's' difficulty knowing how to talk to his son. In constantly returning to the topic of advancing age, Allen and McCabe note that by using 'conversational strategies of confession and listening, bickering and telling jokes, debating and disagreement, the two endlessly discuss the physical signs of ageing and whinge about their growing aches and pains' (Ibid.: 155). The realities of being forty-something and fifty are part of the symbolic journey of *The Trip* as a project. The question that might be asked is how the car becomes a space for the way the two men travel, literally and metaphorically, through each series? More broadly, and extending from this question, what can TV comedy tell us about the sociology of being in cars? Both of these questions turn our attention to the practice of 'passengering'.

## Being together in cars

The concept of passengering is developed by Eric Laurier and Hayden Lorimer in the 'Habitable Cars' project mentioned earlier in this chapter. Focusing on conversations that occur during car journeys, their evidence highlights what is often taken for granted in the way that we travel and 'dwell' in cars, namely the spatial arrangement of speakers and listeners. Rather than arranged face-to-face, people generally sit in cars side-by-side and front-to-back. There is a lack of internal mobility in this context and the inability to step away from a conversation means that occupants of a car must develop ways of talking and interacting that deal with the fixed arrangements of speakers' bodies. Laurier, Lorimer et al. write, 'Regardless of their status, people travelling in the front seats of the car predominantly look out of the windows. This may seem obvious but the point is that the car thereby re-arranges the geometries of our mutual monitoring in ways that can produce a different sort of togetherness' (2008: 11). As anyone who has travelled in a car will know, automotive 'togetherness' can be experienced in different ways; it can involve frustration and delight and possibly both in close quarters if, suddenly, children stop bickering in the back, wayfinding turns from front-seat friction to a B-road found, or the car radio dials from dirge to music gold.[13]

Tellingly, the research team of the Habitable Cars project observed, 'in the car, for family members, colleagues and acquaintances, the geometry of visibility most obviously resembles sitting on the sofa watching television together' (Ibid.: 11). Given the similarity in the arrangement of viewing between cars and TV (eyes forward, side-by-side), it is perhaps unsurprising that television has been drawn to the interior of automobiles as a space of representation. All the examples in this book illuminate the social life of cars, and notably the relation between driver and passenger(s). Examining how drivers' lives take a 'social turn' with passengers beside them, the Habitable Cars project took an ethnographic peek at the way that passengers often get involved in the organisation of the journey and the process of driving. This is performed via gestures and interactions (including 'back-seat' driving) but also through particularities of talk. Laurier, Lorimer et al. note that 'the car remains a small space and its confinement and proximity exert considerable pressure to speak' (Ibid.: 7), leading them to consider the 'distinctiveness of talk-in-cars'. While silences and pauses are clearly part of any car journey, the private space of the car provides a setting where drivers and passengers often look for things to talk about. This is different to public transport, where the 'social expectation of speech is reduced to the point of polite indifference' (Ibid.: 7).

In-car talk provides a rich seam for television comedy, whether filmed in studios against fake road backgrounds or shot on location using rigs and mounted cameras. In situation comedy, car talk often becomes a displacement of the domestic, a site of confined intimacy for character repartee. The comedy drama *Gavin and Stacey*, for example, depicts frequent motorway journeys between the towns of Billericay and Barry Island. Following the romance of two attractive twenty-somethings, each series involves car journeys between England and Wales. These provide comedic and dramatic opportunities for talk between different combinations of parents, siblings, friends and relations. In Series 1, Gavin, his parents and his best friend Smithy (performed by James Corden) play a game called 'cruise, marry, shag' to pass the time on their first journey to Wales, guffawing as they decide which of three celebrities they would rather wed, bed or be confined on a ship with. In a previous episode, Uncle Bryn (performed by Rob Brydon) takes responsibility for driving Stacey, her Mum and her best friend Nessa to Gavin's hometown, partly to try out his new sat-nav. Thanking the device for each new instruction, Bryn regards the sat-nav as a technological marvel, a sentiment that would reverberate in *The Trip to Italy* when 'Brydon' asks 'Coogan' why they have to use physical maps to plot their route when the car can do it for them.

In mixing conventions of drama and comedy, Brett Mills notes that sitcoms like *Gavin and Stacey* 'find humour in observed behaviour rather than jokes' (2009: 128). In-car talk is a facet of

Figure 1.5  Dynamics of passengering, *The Trip to Italy* (2014)

observed behaviour in this context; the programme uses motorways, service stations and drive-thrus to convey the 'different sort of togetherness' afforded by automobiles: battles over music ('do we have to listen to James Blunt all the way?'), the rituals of a roadside stop, transactions that occur in the gap between pay booth and car window, the unbearable tightness of being squashed in cars. The series also involves chat *about* the road, Smithy uncompromising in his view of Chieveley services, located on the M4, as 'sensational'. While the male characters drive, it is notable that Nessa takes charge of an articulated lorry in one episode, participating in motorway trucking culture through the CB radio name 'Robert Mugabe'. When Brydon, as Uncle Bryn, takes the wheel of his Citroen Picasso, his character is often feminised, indicated by his CB radio name of 'Dame Judy Dench'. These tongue-in-cheek subversions point to the way that television comedy plays with gendered hierarchies of driving and passengering even while reinforcing them.

Dynamics of masculinity are worked out in the space of cars and this is especially true in *The Trip* series when it deals with who drives. 'Brydon' is nearly always the passenger and when he does eventually take the wheel of the Mini Cooper in *The Trip to Italy*, 'Coogan' remarks that he drives like a 'district nurse'. The gendering of driving and passengering is made explicit in the very last episode of *The Trip to Greece* ('The Mani to Ithaca') when 'Brydon' remarks that 'there is a psychological disadvantage to being in a passenger seat in a car. The driver automatically assumes higher status'. This leads to a discussion about the emasculation of not being the driver, and the infantilisation of sitting in the back seat. It is notable that when 'Coogan' departs in the last episode and 'Brydon' is joined by his (fictional) wife, it is 'Brydon' who takes the wheel, something he and his wife joke about. The comparison between *Gavin and Stacey* and *The Trip* is useful not only for the way that character elements of Bryn reverberate in the persona of 'Brydon', but also for the way that each series represents in-car talk. While car journeys are a setting in *Gavin and Stacey*, they become an active motif in *The Trip* series. In the former, vehicles are a scene of agreements, disputes, gossip and jokes that advance dramatic storylines about long-distance marriage, birth and the bringing together of families. In the latter, car journeys are a way of emphasising uneventfulness.

According to James Walters, *The Trip* is 'repetitively uneventful, placing its characters in recurring scenarios across an entire series whilst resisting conventional plot development' (2013: 117). Because of this, he suggests that 'slight details such as a glance, a shift in posture, a pause or a sigh take in weight and meaning: they become evidence upon which we base an awareness of and even insights into these people performing a series of apparently minor routines like eating, driving, walking or brushing teeth' (Ibid.: 118). The car journeys in *The Trip* are driving adventures so are not routine in the same way as the commute, discussed in Chapter 3. However, the car journeys are not presented as eventful in themselves. Walters argues that the enjoyment of the driving scenes are in 'Brydon and Coogan's efforts to fill these spaces of "dead" time by amusing one another with imaginative and often comically surreal conversation' (Ibid.: 120). In other words, passengering is the point.

Whether in England, Italy, Spain or Greece, *The Trip* cultivates 'small, delicate portraits of two men amusing each other to pass time between destinations' (Ibid.: 120). The informality of the car is telling on these terms, generating a different register of interaction. Walters observes that the car journeys in the series are distinguished by an improvisatory freedom that the scenes in restaurants do not always have. The car helps convey subtleties in the relation, and exchange, between characters. Sitcoms occasionally transport domestic situations to vehicles as a means of crystallising character interactions. In the British sitcom *Outnumbered* (BBC1, 2007–14), for instance, the programme's portrayal of middle-class family life would sometimes play out in the car. In one episode, the mother (as driver) invites her new age sister, elderly father and three children to play 'who can tell the biggest lie' to pass time in snarled traffic (Series 1, Episode 3). This game precipitates lies of an unruly, outlandish or brutally frank nature ('I like Auntie Angela', says the five-year-old girl sitting in the backseat with her Auntie). Similar to other notable sitcoms like *Modern Family* (ABC, 2009–2020), the depiction of family automobility often bears out the sociology of cars being 'not simply a place for children to argue, get bored, or be transported from A to B; the car is a place for them to learn rules and rights, and how to use, bend, avoid, supplant or break them' (Laurier, Lorimer et al, 2008: 14).[14]

With no immediate domestic scene to transport, *The Trip* generates a more subdued register in the interactions between two male friends. The interior of the car becomes a recurring site for conversations that range and detour. Without being compelled to look at each other directly, as in the restaurants, the two men voice thoughts, comic observations, songs and impersonations that are more stray and less competitive. Shot with functional camera set-ups and editing which follows the direction of speech in the vehicle, car journeys and their conversations are left to meander, leaving the viewer with a frequent sense of eavesdropping. None of the cast in *The Trip* demonstrate awareness of the cameras, distinguishing it from mockumentaries like *Modern Family* which address the audience directly. There is a feeling of voyeurism in the private space of the car, as if the audience is listening to spontaneous talk between the driver and passenger. This is consistent with Michael Winterbottom's disposition towards 'mediated realism', a style that often deliberately complicates a sense of 'truth' and 'representation'.

Although the dialogue of *The Trip* series is substantially improvised, Winterbottom provided skeletons for scenes in each series and would often reshoot sequences many times. Coogan describes the process by saying:

> Michael came to us with a framework of where he wanted the script to go and then we just talk. When he likes something, he'll just wander up and say, 'Do some more of that stuff'. Actually, I wouldn't even call what we were given a script. And I never bother learning it as every day Michael would look at it and say, 'That's not very interesting is it? Let's do something else'. (Jones 2014)

A DVD bonus feature accompanying the first series of *The Trip* shows how the filmmaking process worked to create a sense of improvisation. This includes the rushes of one car scene where 'Coogan' and 'Brydon', inspired by the rugged Yorkshire scenery, riff on how a British costume drama might nail down the precise time and breakfast arrangements for battle the following day. Involving six takes of the same car sequence, Coogan and Brydon do not deliver identical lines, but hit script marks which they embellish and inflect ('Gentlemen, to bed, for we leave at ten-ish'). The rushes show how different cameras are used in separate takes to capture the scene, Brydon at one point telling Coogan to wait ('hang on, we've got a camera issue') and Winterbottom interjecting on the radio to say 'we didn't get that guys'. This points to something obvious but glossed in our willing complicity with TV entertainment: that even when filmed on location in a naturalistic style with a laissez-faire script, television is *produced*. It is the performance of talk and passengering that *The Trip* reveals so nimbly, the conversation in cars being free to roam with signposts.

Reflecting on the evolution of *The Trip* ahead of the fourth instalment, Laura Barton noted in *The Guardian Magazine* that when the programme first launched in 2010 the 'concept demanded a degree of patience on behalf of the viewer', especially with regard to its slowness (2020: 19). While cars often move at speed in TV shows, the uneventful nature of *The Trip* lends itself to a leisurely sense of automotive pace and place. The most significant events to happen in a car throughout the four series are 'Brydon's' navigational stress in the hectic Rome traffic system, and 'Coogan's' solo foray into the Moroccan desert with fuel running low having taken a ferry from Spain. The uneventfulness of *The Trip* links to the series' overarching patterns of repetition: each episode involves a meal, a car journey and the reprising of celebrity impersonations. The car journeys lend themselves to certain types and rhythms of conversation. Talk can linger in a car, but sometimes also drift, shift and tail off. Of course, automobiles can be pressure cookers, and cauldrons of 'road rage', but they can also be contemplative spaces. The journeys in *The Trip* develop this mode of contemplation, giving rise to discussions that range from Baedeker-style primers on the destination ahead to comic reflections on the way Roger Moore might sing pop tunes.

The 'patience' required to watch *The Trip* in each series is also part of the comfort the show offers. As a hybrid sitcom – a 'classy mash-up' of car, food and improvisational genres – it offered a model for other comedy variants of 'slow television'. The idea of slow television develops from the Slow Movement, expressed in manifestos that challenge 'the frantic pace and standardization of contemporary culture' (Berg and Seeber 2016: x). Journeys are ideal subjects for 'slow television' and the term itself was initially used by the Norwegian Public Broadcasting Company in the early 2010s to describe 'minute-by-minute' broadcasts of lengthy Scandinavian train and ship journeys. *Hurtigruten* (NRK2, 2011), for example, was a five-day live broadcast from a cruise ship sailing up the Norwegian coast from Bergen in southern Norway to Kirkenes near the Russian border. Consisting mainly of images from the Norwegian coast – fjords, sunsets and pictures taken from berths while the boat was in harbour – the programme became a national television event, exceeding a million viewers for the last three days of the continuous broadcast.¹⁵ Although *The Trip* was a conventional thirty-minute comedy, it was purposefully unhurried and established a precedent for other British comedies.

There are notable comparisons, for instance, with *Mortimer & Whitehouse: Gone Fishing* (BBC2, 2018–present), a factual entertainment series following the comedians Bob Mortimer and Paul Whitehouse as they drive to various beautiful locations around Britain on fishing excursions.¹⁶ The programme finds two stalwarts of the British comedy scene, known to audiences for three decades (and contemporaries of Coogan and Brydon), coming to terms with middle-age after respective major heart problems. Within its ambient documentary style, conversations meander like the rivers that Mortimer and Whitehouse fish, topics ranging from childhood memories to mid-life ailments. Cars play a bit-part in the series but the programme's mix of scenic beauty and reflective conversation between male friends in the 'autumn of their life' points to a vein of TV commissioning around jokes, journeys and passengering. Having broadcast a six-part series about two famous comedians in 'mid-life hiatus' at the start of the 2010s, BBC2 returned with a different incarnation several years later, which could reasonably be seen as *The Trip* in waders.¹⁷

For some observers, *The Trip* series satirises masculinity. Nigel Morris writes: 'Emphasis on cars, financial power (and ambition and vulnerability), family responsibilities, ageing, anxieties about attractiveness to partners left behind and women encountered – and bedded – on the way, highlights its disquisition on masculinity' (2015: 426). Similarly, James Walters talks of *The Trip*'s 'portrait of male emotional inarticulateness', pointing to the difficulty of communication between the two men beyond their constant impersonations. Walters writes: 'It is especially suitable that situations such as car journeys and restaurant meals should be chosen as environments for this point to be made, given that they contain certain social rules (not making a scene in a restaurant, not making a long journey uncomfortable for a companion) that restrict the opportunities for emotional expression' (2013:

122). The poignancy of *The Trip* lies in its rumination on male middle-age. Cars become a symbolic space and context for this theme.

The last episode of *The Trip to Greece* is especially acute in demonstrating the interactions that cars enable and the emotions they constrain. Playful conversations between the two men about Greek history, the theme tune to *Chariots of Fire* (1981) and the friends' traits as travelling companions ('entertaining but exhausting') turn more serious when 'Coogan' takes a call from his son and learns that his father has died. Unlike *Mortimer & Whitehouse: Gone Fishing*, where the experience of losing a father is shared in the peaceful, pensive flow of a river, *The Trip to Greece* represents the shock of grief in the confined space of a car. For the first time across the series the audience watches 'Coogan' and 'Brydon' drive in silence as aerial shots of the Range Rover traversing beautiful Greek scenery give way to road-level shots of the car stuck in traffic. These sequences build a sense of necessity in 'Coogan', like Odysseus, returning home (something unavailable to the refugees they notice as they catch a car ferry to Cephalonia). While 'Brydon' is met by his wife in Greece and they continue the trip as a marital getaway – 'are you glad I'm here because you get to drive?' she teases – 'Coogan' becomes a passenger in the final scenes, riding silently in the back seat of taxis in Sami and Manchester. To reinforce the symbolic importance of cars, the very last shot of the series is a close-up of 'Coogan' in the back of a cab as he travels to see his father in rest. No longer the driver, his character finally gives up his need for control and the car becomes a space that encloses the gravity of his grief. *The Trip* satirises male middle-age but ends poignantly, the characters driving towards different personal versions of homecoming.

## Conclusion: contemplative comedy

There are many ways that a series like *The Trip* can be examined and TV scholars have used it for different critical purposes, from insights into vocal mimicry (Allen and McCabe 2012) to illustrations of tragi-comedy (Underwood 2015). *The Trip* is not simply concerned with cars. In identifying 'car moments' across the four series it was necessary for me to fast-forward scenes where 'Coogan' and 'Brydon' are sitting in restaurants, making calls in hotels, attempting to exercise or venturing from the vehicle to behold sites of historic interest. Focusing on cars is a selective analytic choice but not, I would argue, a critical whimsy. As an intepretive lens, it provides a way to consider the representation of automobility as a spectacle, situation and form of social practice in contemporary TV comedy.

In her fascinating book *Spectacular Television*, Helen Wheatley examines a new cycle of programmes on British television, emerging in the 2000s, that would dwell on landscape imagery. These included factual entertainment shows like *Coast* (BBC2, 2005–present) that used HD aerial photography to produce spectacular moments of visual pleasure. Focusing on a crossgeneric 'landscape mode' of programing in the mid-late 2000s, Wheatley relates the production economy of shows presenting 'beautiful images in spectacular clarity' with a visual mode where 'narrative progression is frequently slowed or halted to enable contemplative viewing' (2016: 123–36). *The Trip* applied this landscape mode to a form that might be called 'contemplative comedy', a style of slow television where ambient conversation is interspersed with absorbing panoramic scenes.

*The Trip* puts cars in landscapes. More than other examples in this book it combines the spectacular pleasures of HD aerial photography and drone-based camerawork with the visual grammar of car ads attuned to the look, lines and movement of automobiles. The series shifts, however, between stunning panoramas and close-ups inside the car. Coterminous with aerial and road-level views, *The Trip* develops a mode of voyeurism inside vehicles where the audience is made to feel they are eavesdropping on conversations between driver and passenger. The use of location shooting within naturalist sitcom, enabled by the mobility of digital filming, has increased the use of cars as a situation for comedy. Automobiles have become a more regular site of interaction between characters. In examples such as *Better Things, Modern Family, Gavin and Stacey* and *Outnumbered*, the car often functions as a domestic habitat displaced, a space where marital, parental and family dynamics play out in the confinement of the front and back seats, and where women, as mothers, frequently drive.

*The Trip* is about journeys rather than commutes or 'domestic' uses of the car. The series is about middle-aged men taking a life moment and uses the enclosed space of automobiles as a site of talk and reflection in this context. Rather than a confessional space, as in *Marion and Geoff*, the verbal exchanges between 'Coogan' and 'Brydon' capture the contemplative experience of being in cars. This depiction of male hiatus is of course one of class and gender privilege, marked in everything from the type of car and the extravagance of the food to the freedom from parental obligation. To an extent, the programme reflects the 'dominance of masculine comedy' in the history of sitcom (Mills 2009: 21). It is notable that the representation of women in the series is limited to care-giving wives, personal assistants and romantic flings. By comparison, it is rare in the flourishing of 'dramedies' produced, written by and starring (forty-something) women in the 2010s – *Better Things, Catastrophe* (Channel 4, 2015–19), *Motherland* (BBC2, 2016–present) – that any of the lead female characters have time for hiatus. However, *The Trip* is deliberate in dwelling on the anxieties of masculinity, including the toll of advancing age. Rather than equate mid-life crisis with the cliché of flashy coupés, automobiles are used in the series as a space for journeys of personal and celebrity self. *The Trip* represents the practice of passengering as a means to reflect on male friendship and relations forged in the social act of being in cars.

As a product of the 2010s, *The Trip* series is of its time in connecting male adventure to SUVs and a convertible Mini Cooper. These vehicles tap into prevalent marketing images of automobility, linked in the period to aspirational notions of lifestyle and taste. However, the programme is of its time in other ways.

As a co-produced independent project, the journey of *The Trip* from the BBC to Sky and its parallel life as a niche film franchise demonstrate the increasingly fluid boundaries of public service and commercial television, and the blurry distinctions of TV and cinema. The directorial and screen careers of Michael Winterbottom, Steve Coogan and Rob Brydon have moved freely between forms, genres and production cultures within television and film. There is nothing specifically televisual about *The Trip* in its devices, themes or use of cars. It has as many similarities with Alexander Payne's film *Sideways* (2004) – a comedy drama about a road trip by two middle-aged men in California wine country – as it does the representation of masculinity and automobiles in *Top Gear* or *Curb Your Enthusiasm*. Despite allusions in *The Trip* to hierarchies between film and television (expressed in 'Coogan's' professional desire to be seen as a serious film artist rather than a TV personality), the series encapsulates the soft verges of television as a medium. In the next chapter, I consider a particular merging of 'media lanes' in the 2010s. Turning to the 'big thing' in media culture observed by 'Rob Brydon' in *The Trip to Spain*, I examine a phenomenon of car-based entertainment enabled by the rise of digital platforms: 'Carpool Karaoke'.

## 2

# Carpool Karaoke
## On the drive to platforms

The 2010s were a pivotal decade in the digital transformation of television. Not simply a domestic 'box in the corner' delivering programmes through broadcast, cable and satellite, television was increasingly understood as an online service. The development of the internet as a mature distribution channel for film and TV created an ecology of entertainment websites, portals and apps linked to the inexorable rise of 'platforms'. This term is associated with the 'big five' platform corporations (Google, Facebook, Amazon, Apple, Microsoft) that own and operate online services that automate connections between users, content, data and advertising. However, the term also describes platform companies that operate within specific sectors and that often 'disrupt' established industry practices: from booking a taxi using Uber to watching TV through Netflix (van Dijck, Poell and De Wall 2018). If the entwinement of television and internet culture has been driven by platforms, this chapter considers a micro-genre that took 'the drive' literally in the 2010s. Using vehicles as a site for chat, nattering, singing and interviews, passengering became a premise for short-form content highly attuned to the mobile digital environment taking shape. It is perhaps no surprise that in an era of 'platform mobility' (Tryon 2013), where audiovisual media can be produced and consumed on the move, that digital shorts filmed in cars should flourish.

The auto micro-genre in question has taken various forms, from standalone web series and online TV segments to vlogs-in-vehicles by social media 'influencers'. In using the term micro-genre I am not referring to the 'ultra-niche' explored by Molly O'Donnell and Anne Stevens in their anthology *The Microgenre* (2020). Rather than point to the 'obscure and hyper-specific', I refer to content that uses passengering to renew, refresh and refine TV talk show formats. Early examples include web ventures such as Robert Llewellyn's *Carpool* (iTunes/Dave, 2009–14, 2010–11) and Jerry Seinfeld's *Comedians in Cars Getting Coffee* (Crackle/ Netflix, 2012–17, 2017–20). Both series used the habitat of the car as a moving space for conversation with comedians and comic actors, the footage then edited and distributed through streaming platforms. The micro-genre reached its apogee with 'Carpool Karaoke', a recurring segment of *The Late Late Show with James Corden* (CBS, 2015–present). This used carpool commuting as a conceit to fuse talk, singing and skits with a variety of global music stars. Becoming a YouTube phenomenon, 'Carpool Karaoke' moved beyond network television, circulating alongside popular vlogs by the likes of David Dobrik and MrBeast, whose prominent YouTube channels would frequently use cars for pranks and prize give-aways. Demonstrating the *rite of passengering* in the era of social media entertainment, Justin Bieber appeared in three separate 'Carpool Karaoke' videos between 2015 and 2020, as well as in vlogs with Dobrik that involved surprising fans in the back seat of an SUV.

This chapter takes an auto-centric focus to the rise of online comedy entertainment, from Llewellyn's low-tech carpooling and Seinfeld's free-wheeling coffee excursions through to my primary concern with 'Carpool Karaoke', a defining TV-digital hybrid that provides a vantage on the relation between television and YouTube. Before getting to 'Carpool Karaoke' as 'the big thing' in media entertainment in the 2010s (referenced in both *The Trip to Spain* and *Peter Kay's Car Share*), it is helpful to relate the context of platforms to the business of television, especially the emergence of YouTube and Netflix. In the 2010s, these two companies accounted for more than 50 per cent of primetime internet traffic in the US and were ubiquitous across mobile devices in countries around the world, notwithstanding China (Cunningham and

Craig 2019: 21). They provide context for the development and distribution history of the online 'drive-and-talk'.

## The 'drive-and-talk' as online micro-genre

Since launching in 2005 as an online video platform, YouTube has embodied the principle of user interactivity; it is an open service that controls the environment where content is uploaded but that relinquishes control over the content itself. YouTube's early focus on amateur video initially positioned the platform as an alternative to television, a networked space where people could post short videos and 'like', comment and share with a community of users. However, by the late 2000s and early 2010s, YouTube shifted its strategy 'towards viewer-based principles and away from community-oriented social networking' (van Dijck 2013: 117). As a subsidiary of Google, this shift was part of YouTube's attempt to monetise the platform as a space for advertising and included content partnership deals with major TV broadcasters such as NBC, CBS, HBO and the BBC, among others (McDonald 2009). Providing new distribution and promotional opportunities for TV networks, YouTube began to model itself on the flow-like viewing experience of television, redesigning its interface in the late 2000s to encourage viewers to 'stay tuned' for longer periods and with fewer clicks. The increasing volume of professional content on YouTube and the platform's pursuit of advertising led media scholar José van Dijck to write in 2013, 'a far cry from its original design, YouTube is no longer an alternative to television, but a full-fledged player in the media entertainment industry' (2013: 127).

In contrast to the open, interactive and vernacular nature of YouTube, the rise of Netflix in the 2010s represented a different, and more immediate, kind of disruption to established ways of producing, distributing and consuming TV. Evolving from an online movie rental business to a streaming service operating in the US, Netflix began a process of international rollout in the

2010s that transformed the company into the world's largest subscription video-on-demand service (SVOD). According to Catherine Johnson's definition of 'online TV', Netflix is a 'closed and editorially managed' online service that acquires and commissions audiovisual content (2019: 37–8). Unlike YouTube, Netflix provides a portal for accessing and viewing audiovisual media that does not allow users to upload video content or contribute directly to the service.

Writing in 2019, Roman Lobato observed that 'there is still very little agreement about what Netflix *is* or how it should be understood by the public, scholars or media regulators' (2019: 20). In one sense, Netflix can be understood as television in the way it clearly makes and curates professional content that feels like TV and is sold as such. Part of the threat of Netflix to traditional broadcasters has been the company's investment in original content, from high-budget dramas like *The Crown* (2016–present) and *Narcos* (2015–17) to comedies such as *Orange is the New Black* (2013–19). However, Netflix is distinguished not only by its sizeable archive of content – and for promoting 'binge-able' ways of watching it – but through the company's model of gathering data about viewing habits to generate personalised recommendations. It is on these terms that Netflix has positioned itself as a digital media service as much as a TV provider, its vaunted algorithm key to the way that content is customised to individual tastes and preferences.

Robert Llewellyn's *Carpool* and Jerry Seinfeld's *Comedians in Cars Getting Coffee* were both developed and distributed online in the period when YouTube, Netflix and other streaming platforms were coming to the fore. They were conceived as free-to-watch web experiments and grew a dedicated following before their creator-hosts agreed television deals with the UK comedy channel Dave and Netflix, respectively. Developed independently of each other (although Seinfeld apologised for not being aware of Llewellyn's forerunner when copyright claims began to emerge),[1] both series involved established comedians from UK and US sitcoms developing a digital project beyond their TV and stand-up work.

Llewellyn is best known for playing the robot Kryton in *Red Dwarf* (BBC2/Dave, 1988–99, 2009–present), while Seinfeld achieved international fame as the star of the eponymous sitcom, broadcast on NBC between 1989 and 1998. Shifting gear, quite literally, both actors moved away from traditional studio-based sitcoms, thirty minutes in length, towards short-form projects tailored to the new digital environment. Shortly after the launch of *Comedians in Cars Getting Coffee* in 2012, Seinfeld commented:

> This is my personal little idea of a small, fun show, and I think it seems to fit these new mediums: small screens and portable digital platforms. I got the idea at the right time, I guess, because I don't think I could have made this three years ago. I don't think the cameras existed, the viewing devices didn't exist in the numbers that they do now. So it all just kind of seemed to be good timing'. (cited in McGlynn 2012)

Appearing in January 2009, Llewellyn's *Carpool* was developed precisely three years before Seinfeld's 'small, fun show' and was born of a personal interest in the possibilities of online video. Based on the conceit of 'two people in a car having a natter', episodes were released every Friday through iTunes and Llewellyn's YouTube channel. Each episode involved Llewellyn picking up a well-known comedian or TV personality and driving them to a real destination of their choosing: going to the hairdresser (Jo Brand), picking up a script from a TV studio (Craig Charles), buying groceries for a dinner party (David Baddiel), attending a meeting (Jonathan Ross). According to Llewellyn, the series began as an 'experiment to see if there was any truth in all the hype I'd been hearing about new media' (Llewellyn 2010b). Llewellyn talked openly to viewers about the exploratory nature of the project, including the wide-angled bullet cameras that enabled the show to be filmed. These were mounted inside the car pointing at the driver and passenger from the dashboard and back window, with a further camera positioned on the external side of Llewellyn's Toyota Prius. In practical terms, Llewellyn explained that the Prius improved video sound quality as it was a hybrid and therefore quiet. Rarely slow to see a marketing opportunity, Toyota would loan a third-generation Prius for the remainder of the series.

The home-made feel of *Carpool* became part of the novelty of the series. UK television personalities ranging from Stephen Fry and Rob Brydon to the astrophysicist Brian Cox would take a ride with Llewellyn because they knew him professionally or he had given them a call. Until the series was picked up by the male-targeted channel Dave (branded as 'the home of witty banter'), Llewellyn booked the guests, picked them up and recorded, edited, uploaded and promoted the series as a solo endeavour. As if to reinforce the hobbyist nature of the show, four episodes were filmed but not released due to prosaic technical errors caused by Llewellyn, from inaudible sound to a flat camera battery. While Llewellyn is part of the formal creative industries, with established links in the television business, *Carpool* was informal in its digital creation and circulation. Neither professional nor amateur in a complete sense, and lasting between 12 and 20 minutes in length, *Carpool* occupied a space between a TV programme and the 'ephemeral' clips and videos that abound on YouTube (Grainge 2011).

According to Ramon Lobato and Julian Thomas, one of the potential functions of 'informal media', intentionally or not, is to incubate ideas that are then taken up by formal media industries (2015: 30). Such was the case with *Carpool*, one of the first shows, in Llewellyn's words, to start life on the internet and end up on 'proper telly', in this case a non-terrestrial channel aimed at men aged 16–44. In a video 'update' to his online followers, Llewellyn explained that the deal with Dave provided the technical and production support needed to make and distribute the show on a weekly basis. Broadcasting extended versions of the show, Llewellyn was keen to reassure online viewers that *Carpool* would also continue to be released through iTunes and YouTube, maintaining three key features: the episodes would be in high definition, small enough to go on a phone and would be available in 'audio only' versions. These features are characteristic of the video podcast and point to the way that digital content is not only viewed on smartphones but also heard through connected devices, ideal entertainment when driving a car (Llewellyn 2010c).

As a web experiment, *Carpool* often includes repartee between driver and passenger on the nature of filming and talking in cars. Busy in conversation, passengers sometimes ask 'are we filming?' or 'is the camera on?'. Llewellyn's *Red Dwarf* co-star Craig Charles joked, 'are people really going to watch this shit?' More reflectively, the comedian David Baddiel ruminates on the nature of his conversation with Llewellyn, commenting, 'I wonder what the car gives it?' Excited by the question, Llewellyn extemporises on the way that people converse in a car, saying 'what you tend to do at home or in a studio is you've two chairs and you angle them in a weird crap way and it's automatically unnatural' (Llewellyn 2010a). For Llewellyn, it is the forward-facing nature of the driver and passenger that makes for greater naturalism in car conversation, what he refers to as 'the thing that happens when you're driving with someone'. Jerry Seinfeld makes a similar point about the informality of automotive talk in *Comedians in Cars Getting Coffee*, wryly commenting to the talk show host Jay Leno – his passenger on a drive that includes meandering chat about age, career and being a comedian – 'you can't have a conversation like this in a real interview'. Offering a mobile space for the celebrity interview, the informality of the car helps facilitate intimacy of a kind less possible in a TV studio.

As a web series developed by the co-creator and star of one of the most successful sitcoms in American television history (Kalyan 2019), Seinfeld's 'small fun show' was of a different scale to *Carpool*. While Llewellyn's *Carpool* YouTube channel achieved five million views over a period of a decade, episodes of Seinfeld's car series were streamed nearly 100 million times in its first three years (Itzkoff 2015). *Comedians in Cars Getting Coffee* was nominated for Primetime Emmy Awards in the categories of 'Outstanding Short-format Nonfiction Program' (2013, 2014), 'Outstanding Variety Talk Series' (2016), 'Outstanding

Informational Series or Special' (2019) and 'Outstanding Hosted Nonfiction Series or Special' (2020). The series was released weekly on Thursday nights on the show's website and on a free video streaming platform called Crackle, co-owned by Sony Pictures Television. Unlike *Carpool*, which was distinctly user-generated in feel, *Comedians in Cars Getting Coffee* was professionally made, managed and distributed from the outset, a 'personal' project with a far more significant budget ($100k per episode) and extensive brand value in the market of online and SVOD content.

According to Seinfeld, the web series was designed as an 'anti-show about a non-event' (McGlynn 2014). The title sequence of *Comedians in Cars Getting Coffee* includes a pencil-drawn logo, framing the series as something of a doodle. In each episode, Seinfeld calls an old friend or acquaintance from the comedy scene, picks them up in a vehicle taken to embody the guest, and drives them to get coffee. Episodes last anywhere between 12 and 23 minutes and involve three principal set-ups: the pick-up and drive, the stroll and coffee, and the return drive. Much like *The Trip*, discussed in Chapter 1, the main scenes are either in a car or at a table drinking and eating. In an interview with David Letterman promoting the fourth series, Seinfeld explained the importance of cars by saying: 'part of what makes the show watchable is that it's always moving. There's no narrative [to] drive the story. We know what happens. We know they're going to get coffee. You need a kinetic energy to move it along. Moving people around keeps them awake' (McGlynn 2014). On these terms, the car provides opportunities for driver and passenger to riff, gaze, press switches on the dashboard and comment on 'the ride'. Like *Carpool*, the road provides impromptu material, from occasions when the car in question has mechanical issues ('have you done the car breaking down bit before?' asks Steve Martin, looking at their 1954 Siata 8V stranded in a layby) to situations when Seinfeld speaks to other drivers from the window of the vehicle ('we're doing the Seinfeld reunion and you're not in it', Jerry says jokingly to a woman whose parked car is obstructing the 1964 Aston Martin DB5 he is driving with Julia Louis-Dreyfus).

Cars form part of the identity of each episode. This is established in the titles where Seinfeld introduces both vehicle and guest, providing the specification and history of the automobile and a statement that links the personality of the vehicle to that of the passenger. The titles involve interior and exterior close-ups of the automobile (the ignition, gear stick, wheel rims, seat fabric, bumpers), over which Seinfeld provides a voice-over detailing the horsepower, engine size, logbook colour ('signal red', 'opalescent blue') and a more poetic assessment of character: 'this is a car for guys who want a sports car but don't want to be inconvenienced' (1970 Mercedes-Benz W113, Alec Baldwin), 'if you feel like me that humility is in short supply, this is the car for you' (1952 Volkswagen Beetle, Larry David). Establishing a phone set-up that contrives the drive ('are you free?') and a scene that unveils the car to the passenger, the programme is fashioned around a vehicle, normally a classic model from the 1950s, 60s or 70s borrowed for the day from a private owner. While the show was sponsored by Acura, the luxury vehicle division of Honda, only one Acura ever featured. Guests often share feelings about the car in question, but equally offer thoughts about coffee with quick cuts to beans, espresso machines and foam flourishes, all set to jaunty jazz music.

The 'non-event' in question is an everyday pursuit: driving, talking, getting a coffee. The fact that *the drive* is in a classic car and *the talk* is with a famous comedian (Tina Fey, Jon Stewart, Eddie Murphy, Sarah Silverman among eighty others over eleven seasons) established a context for one of television's most celebrated proponents of comedy about the mundane – *Seinfeld*, often described as a 'show about nothing' (Kalyan 2020) – to establish a portrait of the quotidian among stars. Cars were central to the aim of giving 'fans a taste of what it means to live a life in comedy, specifically the casual chatter that enriches it' (McGlynn 2012). Removing the lure for comedians to perform an 'act' in front of a studio audience, *Comedians in Cars Getting Coffee* was an experiment, like *Carpool*, in creating a 'certain mood' through vehicles.

**Figure 2.1** Feeling the car, *Comedians in Cars Getting Coffee* (2019)

Similar to Llewellyn, Seinfeld spoke of the labour involved in making short-form content, in particular the work of editing three hours of material into fifteen minutes that could maintain people's attention online. Describing the creative process, he noted, 'it may seem completely casual, and the day is casual, but the post-production is not casual because I want these shows to have this particular feeling' (Ibid.). The idea of feeling is apt. Writing about the experience of 'feeling the car' – 'how people feel *about* and *in* cars, and how the feel of different car cultures elicits specific dispositions and ways of life' – Mimi Sheller invites us to think about the 'co-constitution of motion and emotion' (2004: 224–6). 'Feeling the car' is part of the tenor of *Comedians in Cars Getting Coffee*. The establishing monologue, introducing the specification and personality of a vehicle in a time and place, is a paean to the sensuality of motoring.

Explaining to David Letterman why he made *Comedians in Cars Getting Coffee* as a web series, rather than a network or cable television show, Seinfeld remarked, 'I was thinking, what would be a good TV show for a phone?' (McGlynn 2014). Cars became a way of moving beyond the 'controlled environment' of formal television in this context. For Seinfeld, control refers not only to the studio-based nature of filming but also, one might infer, to the rigmarole of developing a conventional TV series. Like *Carpool*, the show was geared to a culture of mobile viewing. In the words of one TV critic, it offered 'a nice little diversion; something to watch at your desk while you ate a sandwich at work' (Heritage 2019). It was a sign of the rise of online TV in the 2010s that a series that began as a web short – what Seinfeld championed as 'something in your pocket, for free' (Itzkoff 2015) – led to a deal with Netflix worth $100 million.

According to Nick Marx, the hypercompetitive nature of the US cable and digital TV market in the 2010s led TV providers to view comedy 'as a way both to stand out from the pack and to attract young male viewers' (2018: 180). Netflix was part of this industry mode of thinking. Using the internet to 'taste-test' consumer appetite for Seinfeld's 'anti-show about a non-event' (Lobato and Thomas 2015: 31), Netflix signed a deal in 2017 for twenty-four new episodes of *Comedians in Cars Getting Coffee*, along with the back catalogue of the web series and two Seinfeld stand-up specials. Netflix provides a 'non-linear' viewing experience, meaning it is not governed by a schedule organised in 'day parts' (morning, afternoon, primetime, late-night) offering programmes of fixed lengths (30, 60, 90 minutes). As users construct their own sequences of viewing on Netflix, shaped by algorithmic recommendations, the duration of a show is less important than its ability to appeal to groupings of taste. *Comedians in Cars Getting Coffee* tapped different potential taste preferences: a marquee name in US television doing celebrity interviews in a car format with lifestyle features.[2] From its origins as a web series, the words in the title alone – Comedians, Cars, Coffee – seemed perfectly fashioned for the culture of algorithmic search.

By its own account, *Comedians in Cars Getting Coffee* influenced many variations of the 'drive-and-talk' format in the 2010s. The Netflix trailer for the eleventh season in 2019 went as far as to list 'knock-offs the show has inspired', reeling names of (mainly YouTube) talk-based shows and comic parodies such as 'Clergy in Cars Getting Coffee', 'Cougars in Cars Getting Cosmos', 'Politicians in Cars Getting Coffee', 'Comedians on Bikes Getting

Soup', 'Funny Uber Rides', 'Alec Baldwin's Love Rides' and, notably, 'Carpool Karaoke'. The 'drive-and-talk' became a highly flexible micro-genre, from pastors in cars discussing theological topics to Hollywood stars giving relationship advice from the back of a cab. These all used mobile video equipment to create accessible, auto-centric short-forms.

That 'Carpool Karaoke' appeared first in the list of 'imitators' is playful (if not rich) given that *Comedians in Cars Getting Coffee* might be viewed as a caffeinated version of Robert Llewellyn's series. In fact, 'Carpool Karaoke' was based on a BBC Comic Relief sketch that Corden performed with George Michael in 2011, the year before Seinfeld turned his first ignition key. And yet, Corden's late night segment did echo the dashboard aesthetics of web-based shows and vlogs that were coming to the fore; it was part of a trend in the 2010s for reframing 'the vehicle as a performative space of intimate dialogue with the audience in the space of daily activity' (McNutt 2017: 581). Having established a context for an emergent online genre, I consider the nature of the vehicle as performative space in the most prominent TV-digital example of its kind.

## Carpool Karaoke as television and digital media

The late-night talk show is a staple of American network television. Driven by the personality of their hosts – David Letterman, Jimmy Kimmel, Jay Leno, Stephen Colbert, Jimmy Fallon, James Corden, among other custodians of '*Late*' or '*Late Late*' programmes by NBC, CBS and ABC – entertainment talk shows are designed to amuse. Jeffrey P. Jones observes that late-night talk is 'a highly segmented programming form, including a comedic monologue, comedy sketches, video vignettes, musical performances, and celebrity guest interviews [where] most comedian hosts have perfected some sort of signature comedy piece that is prominently and repeatedly offered' (2009: 18). In presenting a range of short segments, the late-night talk show was well placed to respond to digital media transitions in the 2000s and 2010s. Adapting to the new screen ecology of websites, portals and apps, networks used flagship entertainment shows to provide clips and snippets that were unbundled from the broadcast programme and spread widely across digital platforms. The 'video vignette' became increasingly significant in this context, a segment of the talk show that could circulate on YouTube as a digital short with a life and status of its own.

'Carpool Karaoke' is one of the most successful examples of a late-night talk show becoming a regular generator of digital content. The segment made its first appearance in March 2015 as part of the launch of *The Late Late Show with James Corden* (CBS, 2015–present). Taking a gamble on the choice of Corden as host – an actor, singer and comedy writer largely unknown outside the UK – the revamped CBS talk show was differentiated through digital means.[3] Airing in the post-midnight slot of the US broadcast schedule, *The Late Late Show* established itself anew by embracing YouTube, creating features like 'Carpool Karaoke' that were internet-friendly in length and address.

Examining late-night television's 'digital turn', Myles McNutt contends that programmes like *The Tonight Show Starring Jimmy Fallon* (NBC, 2014–present) and *The Late Late Show with James Corden* deliberately sought to expand their viewership beyond the broadcast audience, focusing from the outset on the 'successful translation of late-night programming into the nonlinear distribution logics of the YouTube platform' (2017: 570). Between March 2015 and June 2017, *The Late Late Show*'s YouTube channel grew from 27,000 subscribers to 11.3 million, far outstripping the show's broadcast audience, which averaged 1.34 million viewers in the 2016–17 season (Ibid.: 579). 'Carpool Karaoke' was instrumental in this growth, helping to generate 1.7 billion worldwide views on YouTube in the first seventeen months of the show's launch (Sweney 2016). Corden's drive-and-sing with Adele, the most watched of all 'Carpool Karaoke' videos, amassed 42 million views within the first five days of being posted.[4]

These numbers fuelled industry debate about how programme success should be measured in the TV business. The standard metric, used to set the price of advertising, has traditionally been ratings, the gauge of how many people watch a live broadcast. Although online 'catch-up' has become part of contemporary viewing calculations, ratings do not account for more complex forms of online engagement. Reflecting this point, executive producer of *The Late Late Show*, Ben Winston, told the Edinburgh Television Festival in 2016: 'When I get in in the morning I will check our YouTube hits before I check our overnights [ratings]. The overnights just tell us who managed to stay awake. The YouTube hits tell us which bits flew' (cited in Sweney 2016). Corden expanded:

> I genuinely couldn't tell you how many people watch our show, because I feel like in this slot, *we're not really in the ratings business, we're just in the relevance business*. My major ambition is just to stay relevant. That's it, to be in the conversation – that's all that was ever asked of us really. (Ibid., my italics)

These pronouncements were borne of the growing realignment between television and digital media in the 2010s. This includes the cross-pollination of media forms but also the models and metrics that support ways of doing business in the 'post-network' era.

Anthologies in contemporary TV studies like *Television as Digital Media* (Bennett and Strange 2011) and *From Networks to Netflix* (Johnson 2018) remind us that 'television' is not a single category, or a technology leading to some inexorable convergence with the internet. While the shift to digital has challenged long-held assumptions about television as a medium, there is little to be gained from deciding whether a phenomenon like 'Carpool Karaoke' belongs, more properly, to the world of 'television' or 'digital media'. In form and distribution, it is a hybrid. It was conceived as part of a TV programme but built with YouTube in mind; it was developed to grow and promote a late-night franchise but also became a digital show of its own. Myles McNutt considers the way that segments like 'Carpool Karaoke' and other YouTube-friendly features such as Jimmy Fallon's 'Classroom Instruments' (the host collaborating with music stars to perform their songs on xylophones and tambourines) were 're-ritualized' for the platform environment (2017: 576). This describes how late-night talk shows developed video content that could be reframed outside of the linear broadcast context.

This process of re-framing would include the use of online trailers and thumbnails on YouTube channels that positioned Corden and Fallon as YouTube creators rather than TV talk show hosts. 'Carpool Karaoke' also made use of customised 'end tags' when videos were posted online. Addressed to the YouTube audience and recorded in the car, these tags would thank the viewer for watching, direct users to other 'Carpool Karaoke' videos and push the audience to subscribe to the YouTube channel. There are few explicit references to *The Late Late Show* in these moments. The web content was positioned as a standalone brand, with YouTube figured 'as the primary space of engagement for the "Carpool Karaoke" audience' (Ibid.: 583). In business terms, the number of YouTube views for 'Carpool Karaoke' enabled CBS to leverage more lucrative sponsor deals than would have been possible based on TV ratings. This included a product integration deal with McDonald's that involved Corden using a drive-thru to order French fries and Cokes with Selena Gomez as passenger.[5] More significantly, the attempt to monetise 'Carpool Karaoke' led to a licensing deal with Apple Music for a digital spin-off called *Carpool Karaoke: The Series*. This version premiered on Apple Music in 2017 and on the newly launched Apple TV a year later. Although produced by CBS and Fulwell 73 (Ben Winston's production company), the on-demand version of the series did not use Corden but instead featured different combinations of celebrity driver/passenger John Cena and Shaquille O'Neal in one episode, Kendall Jenner and Hailey Bieber in the next.

McNutt notes the 'equal standing' between television and YouTube in the contemporary distribution of late-night TV. He suggests that 'a space originally used as a "second-window" for Fallon and Corden has increasingly emerged as a first window for late-night content, solidifying and growing the cultural footprint of late-night talk shows in a contemporary television landscape despite linear ratings declines' (2017: 585). Corden's claim to be in the 'relevance business' rather than the 'ratings business' can be set in this context; the comment would speak to the impetus for sharing content and being 'in the conversation' on social media platforms. But why the relevance of cars in this case? On what terms did the 'drive-and-talk' – or more accurately the 'drive-and-sing' – become a pertinent form of content to share and spread? This invites a closer look inside the vehicle.

'Carpool Karaoke' uses the conceit of Corden being late for work at CBS studios and needing a passenger to use the carpool lane. Thanking the (as yet unseen) passenger beside him, a music star is revealed in the adjacent seat. The first six 'drives' featured Mariah Carey, Jennifer Hudson, Justin Bieber, Iggy Azalea, Rod Stewart and Stevie Wonder. Gaining celebrity traction, segments were subsequently filmed in London (Adele), Liverpool (Paul McCartney), New York (Madonna) and Las Vegas (Celine Dion), and sometimes featured multiple stars at once (Gwen Stefani joined by George Clooney and Julia Roberts). Filmed in a Range Rover – once again the celebrity auto-du-jour, as in *The Trip* – the segment is based on Corden and passenger singing in-car versions of the music star's famous hits. Between these moments, Corden engages in interview-lite chat, sometimes integrating a comedy sketch inside or outside the vehicle.

To illustrate, the segment with Stevie Wonder begins with a skit where Corden, anxious in the passenger seat, asks the unknown driver 'are you sure you're okay to drive?' Revealing Stevie Wonder, the gag continues with front seat discussion about seat belts and the whereabouts of Wonder's driving licence, the singer clearly enjoying the joke (mimicking an English accent and Corden acting displeasure at being 'wound up'). Switching seat positions, the drive itself involves the pair singing along to six of Wonder's hits as they play on the car stereo. This is interspersed

Figure 2.2 'I just called to say James loves you', Stevie Wonder in 'Carpool Karaoke' (2015)

with Wonder using Facetime to call friends and acquaintances, doing Corden 'a favour' by calling his wife, the host visibly tearful when Wonder sings 'I just called to say James loves you'. The drive is filmed through cameras mounted on the dashboard, with occasional medium range intercuts showing the back of the SUV driving around Los Angeles. The segment lasts ten minutes.

As signifiers of consumer culture, automobiles have long been a feature of the music videos that circulate on channels like MTV and platforms such as YouTube. The 2009 video for 'Music' by Madonna, for example, is filmed in a limousine chauffeured by the character of Ali G, Madonna handing the hapless driver a gold CD so she can sing, drink and party in the back. Watching stars like Madonna and Lady Gaga perform songs in the less-than-glamorous act of commuting made 'Carpool Karaoke' distinct, and humorous, in the YouTube search environment. While my own search tendency would be to find a particular 'Carpool Karaoke' video (say Red Hot Chili Peppers) and watch it from start to finish, my sixteen-year-old son's encounter with 'Carpool Karaoke' was different; he was more inclined to watch abbreviated 'Carpool Karaoke' clips when these appeared as YouTube recommendations beside music artists he liked (say the hip hop trio Migos).

Whatever the individual viewing habits on YouTube, 'Carpool Karaoke' made itself visible on the platform across musical and generational lines. Featuring passengers from Usher to Elton John, Kanye West to Chris Martin, the fascination of stars in cars, engaged in a singalong, gave the videos wide appeal for sharing. Henry Jenkins, Sam Ford and Joshua Green argue that for media content to spread it has to be 'portable', 'quotable' and 'grabbable' (2013: 198). 'Carpool Karaoke' embodied these elements in aesthetic terms. While commuting is inherently portable, karaoke enacts the quotable. As short-form comedy entertainment, 'Carpool Karaoke' not only inscribed a sense of mobility, the videos lent themselves to being grabbed and viewed on the go.

In their ethnographic study of passengering, introduced in Chapter 1, Laurier, Lorimer et al. suggest that when sharing a car journey to work the driver is 'put in the position of host towards the passenger' (Laurier, Lorimer et al. 2008: 15). Based on video recordings of carpool journeys, their study observes: 'in limited ways, the driver, who is ordinarily the owner of the car, receives the passenger (in that they are in the car first) and becomes responsible for the welfare and comfort of their guest' (Ibid.: 15). Assuming 'proprietary control over what are acceptable habits for shared travel', Laurier, Lorimer et al. note that drivers 'are normally responsible for entertainment which is usually and simply the radio/CD player'. Although writing before smartphones and music streaming sidelined CDs in cars and elsewhere, the idea of the driver as host is useful as it is made literal in 'Carpool Karaoke'. The segment explicitly places the show's entertainment host within a vehicle, Corden 'receiving' the passenger-as-guest, making them comfortable and taking responsibility for entertainment in the selection of songs.

Like the other case examples in this book, 'Carpool Karaoke' creates a sense of intimacy in the confined space of the automobile. The format offered new opportunities for celebrities to present themselves in this context; the situation of the car allowed stars to convey a more informal persona and also to perform older, fan-beloved hits. According to Ben Winston, 'you're not getting Britney Spears on *The Late Late Show* and she's singing Hit Me Baby One More Time. Imagine telling the publicist that is what you wanted. Whereas with Carpool Karaoke we'll just put their greatest hits in there. Which is why it works' (Sweney 2016). 'Carpool Karaoke' would provide a different format to the late-night celebrity talk and plug. Instead, we see Stevie Wonder's mischievous capacity for faux English accents before he and Corden sing along to 'Superstition' in a moving SUV. Or we watch Jennifer Lopez and Corden sing a version of 'Jenny From the Block' before they park up and we discover the list of celebrity contacts in 'J-Lo's' smartphone, witnessing her seemingly genuine mortification when Corden sends a prank message to her friend Leonardo DiCaprio.

As driver-host, Corden brings an 'everyman' quality to the role; he often exhibits thrill and disbelief that he is singing along to famous songs performed by (and beside) his passenger. With global stars like Stevie Wonder and Paul McCartney, Corden's fannish enthusiasm leads to emotional welling when he sings along to iconic hits like The Beatles' 'Let it Be'. Despite his credentials as a performer with BAFTA, Tony and Emmy Awards, Corden's emerging star persona in the US was based on his unassuming style.[6] Similar to the character of Smithy, the tracksuit-wearing builder from *Gavin and Stacey* who would drive and sing with George Michael in a three-minute charity sketch for Comic Relief, it was plausible to believe that Corden might drive around harmonising to hits by Wham! and Coldplay. Despite the staging, 'Carpool Karaoke' played on the guise of authenticity in famous people doing everyday things, in this case driving to work and singing in cars.

In January 2020, a minor social media storm erupted around 'Carpool Karaoke' after a fan posted a video on Twitter of Corden's SUV being towed by a rig (a truck with a camera) while filming an episode with Justin Bieber. The footage led to claims of 'Carpool Karaoke' being 'a con' in revealing that Corden did not always drive the vehicle in question. Ben Winston issued a disclaimer on Twitter, exclaiming 'Not true! We only use a rig when we are doing a "stunt" as part of the Carpool – when it would be impossible for James to drive!'. This was followed by a tongue-in-cheek rejoinder on *The Late Late Show*'s official Twitter account, showing a picture of Corden and Samuel L. Jackson sitting behind a toy driving wheel in a spoof of *Pulp Fiction* (1994) with the caption, 'guys, we don't even use a real car'. Although laughing off claims of fakery, the brouhaha was telling as it threw into relief the blurred status of 'Carpool Karaoke' as television and 'social media entertainment'.

Stuart Cunningham and David Craig argue that social media entertainment (which they abbreviate to SME) is defined by 'intensely normative discourses of authenticity' (2019: 3). By their definition, social media entertainment describes a 'proto-industry' of content creators and intermediaries who operate through interactive platforms such as YouTube, Twitter, Facebook, Instagram, Snapchat and Chinese equivalents like Youku, Weibo and WeChat. Cunningham and Craig describe this proto-industry as 'fueled by professionalizing, previously amateur content creators using new entertainment and communicative formats, including vlogging, gameplay, and do-it-yourself (DIY), to develop potentially sustainable businesses based on significant followings that can extend across multiple platforms' (Ibid.: 5). Vlogging is arguably the core format in this list, used by social media 'influencers' to interact with followers. Among settings, this can include vlogs inside vehicles.[7]

Cunningham and Craig suggest that the discourse of authenticity and community defines the distinctive mode of social media entertainment. Eschewing artifice in the staging and scripting of videos, intimacy in vlogging is often enhanced by the vlogger's proximity to the camera. Cars provide an especially close and confined space for talking to viewers in this context. To take an example, the first video posted on the family-oriented *Dad V Girls* vlog channel in 2018 – focusing on challenges and games between a Dad (Joel Conder) and his wife and four daughters – featured a car trip to a safari park. Filmed inside the Conders' people carrier, the family in question talk to the dashboard camera, creating a

**Figure 2.3** Vlogging in vehicles, *Dad V Girls* (2018). From the *Dad V Girls* YouTube channel, https://www.youtube.com/watch?v=xgy_WHe_NRs (last accessed 12 July 2021)

feeling of intimacy through the way the parents and children chat, joke, challenge Dad to remember their sandwich requests, notice people in other cars and drive through the safari grounds.

The family members contribute to a video diary in a manner that establishes them all as relatable characters, propelling *Dad V Girls* to a million subscribers in its first two years. A popular meme such as 'Chewbacca Mom', a short video that went viral in 2016, provides a different example of home-made car intimacy. An amateur video of a mother putting on a toy mask in the front seat of her car, and laughing uproariously, the clip spread widely on social media. The infectious joy of the Mom (Candace Payne) wearing her child's *Star Wars* mask while parked received so much exposure that it led James Corden to invite Payne onto *The Late Late Show*, momentarily bringing together the stars of spreadable car-based entertainment.

It was the breach of trust in 'Carpool Karaoke's' effect of intimacy that brought a backlash of sorts. As a creation of the television industry, the segment involved the production support one might expect filming on location in a large vehicle with a famous star.[8] There was no pretence that the drive was spontaneous, unscripted or shot without a film crew. However, the segment tapped into vernacular styles of vlogging through its dashcam aesthetic and guise of informality. The 'faked' drive in question involved Justin Bieber and James Corden creating a TikTok dance in the front seat of the car that obliged Corden, briefly, to remove his hands from the driving wheel. In choreographing dance moves that spoke 'relevance' to one social media platform (TikTok), the segment used a tow-truck that questioned the 'authenticity' of its vlog-style address on another (YouTube).

As a TV-digital hybrid, the content status of 'Carpool Karaoke' varied depending on the context of distribution. At one level, 'Carpool Karaoke' became a paratext, a strategic promotional form that helped create and amplify meanings of the *The Late Late Show* as the 'primary' network vehicle (Gray 2010). However, the segment also developed its own identity and following. Elizabeth Evans (2018) notes that it was the success of 'Carpool Karaoke' on YouTube that led to distribution deals for *The Late Late Show* outside the US. In the UK, for example, Sky acquired broadcast rights to the programme and aired a 'Carpool Karaoke' Special on its Sky1 channel in 2016. Meanwhile, the German free-to-air broadcaster RTL began showing un-dubbed episodes a day after the US airing. In parallel, as mentioned previously, a licensing deal was signed with on-demand provider Apple TV to make *Carpool Karaoke: The Series*. This accompanied separate format deals for versions in TV markets with local hosts and featuring music stars beyond North America and the UK. These included *Carpool Karaoke Italia* (2017), broadcast on Italia1 and hosted by the Italian rapper Jake Le Furia, and *Carpool Karaoke Arabia* (2018), shown on Dubai TV and hosted by Saudi singer Hisham Al-Howaish.

'Carpool Karaoke' adapted successfully across media markets. This owed in part to the way the series tuned into the global popularity of music performance on YouTube and social networking services. However, the underlying conceit of car passengering also translated well in different national contexts. Translation, here, can be understood in both cultural and figurative terms.

Tim Edensor writes of the 'national resonances of car cultures' (2004: 103), reminding us that not all forms of automobility are the same. Rather than feature a fortress-like SUV, the Italian version of 'Carpool Karaoke' was filmed in a compact Fiat 500. *Carpool Karaoke Italia* made the format culturally resonant by using a small 'city car' and having passenger-guests perform Italian musical favourites. In one episode, for instance, the operatic pop trio Il Volo sing their own hits but also perform exuberant versions of classic Italian opera as well as football anthems, occasionally bursting from the vehicle (when stationary) to sing in the road.

Translation can also be understood figuratively, however. Whether using an oversized Range Rover or an apportioned Fiat, the concept of car-based karaoke was ideally suited to an era where media is portable, sociality is performed, and audiences are on the move. The series translated well, in short, to a culture of media mobility. Having established the status of 'Carpool Karaoke' as a TV-digital hybrid, I consider in more detail the inclination to perform in the space of the automobile. In the next section, I turn to the representation of an act that people in vehicles occasionally, but not uncommonly, catch themselves doing – singing.

## Singing and the sonic world of cars

Michael Bull describes the car as the ideal 'personalized listening environment' (2004: 247). Unlike domestic spaces that vary in size and shape, cars offer uniformity in acoustic design. Sound historians have discussed how automobiles have been turned into 'mobile listening booths' in the last hundred years, moving from the noisy vehicles of early development to today's 'sonic capsules' that feel 'acoustically sealed off from the outside world' (Bijsterveld, Cleophas and Krebs 2013: 2). From the material construction of engines, bodies, wipers, blinkers and tyres that reduce sound and dampen noise outside the car, to the pin-sharp audio systems and digital speakers that bring music, radio, podcasts and traffic information inside the vehicle, the modern automobile has been designed with a mind to 'acoustic cocooning' (Ibid.: 2).

Sound encapsulates the duality of public and private in the experience of automobility; cars enable people to move about in public space but within a privatised environment. Considering the way that individuals use sound and music while on the move, Michael Bull comments:

> An increasing number of us demand the intoxicating mixture of noise, proximity and privacy while on the move and have the technologies to precisely and successfully achieve these aims. The use of these largely sound technologies informs us about how we attempt to 'inhabit' the spaces within which we live. (2004: 243)

According to Bull, mediated sound becomes a way of 'inhabiting' the automobile and can be regarded as a component of what it is to drive. Having chosen a track, a radio station or a podcast to play in the car, drivers 'construct visual space according to a privatized soundworld' (Ibid.: 248). As with 'Coogan's' choice of Joy Division for the soundtrack of the Yorkshire Dales, discussed in Chapter 1, the drives we take are framed by the sounds we select. Whether music, radio or the voice of a sat-nav, sound qualitatively changes the experience of automobility.

This can engender different moods and behaviours inside the car. Bijsterveld el al. note that many people view their vehicle as a place to 'unwind' during in-between moments of the day. They give the example of commuters who might enjoy a 'peaceful moment' for themselves between the demands of work and the chores of home (2013: 3). Equally, the car can become a space of performance where drivers feel enabled to sing in their acoustic cocoon. In the US sitcom *The Big Bang Theory* (CBS, 2007–19), an episode in Season 5 shows the character of nerd-scientist Leonard driving alone, singing along weakly but sincerely to 'I've Got a Feeling' by the Black Eyed Peas ('The Vacation Solution'). Leonard sings without inhibition until his flatmate Sheldon reveals himself in the back seat with the proclamation, 'Good lord, will you stop that caterwauling'. Michael Bull observes: 'the space of a car is both one to look out from and to be looked in to. It is simultaneously private and public. Drivers both lose themselves in the pleasure of habitation and may also become increasingly aware of the 'look' of others' (2004: 249). In the example from *The Big Bang Theory*, the seclusion of automotive singing is undermined from within, the 'look of others' coming not from adjacent motorists pulling up beside the car but from a stowaway in the rear.[9]

The immersion of sound in cars can be a solo experience but also a social one. 'Carpool Karaoke' relies on the combination of two or more people in a vehicle as host and guest. The word 'karaoke' is significant in this context. Invented in Japan in the 1970s and popularised in bars across the world in the 1980s, the film historian Barbara Klinger defines karaoke as 'the art of singing in the shower writ into public space' (2006: 183). Focusing on amateurs who sing a familiar song with recorded musical accompaniment in front of an audience, there is a highly performative aspect to karaoke, whether undertaken alone or with others.

As a practice, karaoke can involve sincere but also ironic musical expression, 'one can pursue a "mimetic" performance in all seriousness, but also parody the songs' (Peters, van Eijck and Michael 2018: 62). Part of the fascination of 'Carpool Karaoke' is the spectacle of music stars singing along to their own songs, neither entirely seriously nor engaged in parody. As driver, Corden controls the environment of the automobile through the selection of music, asking passengers if they mind if he puts on some tunes, or posing the leading question, 'shall we see what's on the radio'? This prompts the car's audio system to play one of the guest's famous hits, whereupon driver and passenger sing along in the front seats, sometimes choreographing an upper body dance. In certain cases, artists pose and sing directly to the in-car camera as if the karaoke element of the drive is a music video (Madonna). Occasionally, another passenger will appear in the back seat to sing or rap at a key moment (the rapper A$AP briefly joins in the back seat during the drive with Rod Stewart). In most cases, however, guests sing as they might during a regular car ride, looking ahead and out of the window. The nature of singing is never 'caterwauling' but 'Carpool Karaoke' approximates the car as a scene where driver and passenger are singing along for their own pleasure in a shared private space.

While Corden and guest generally 'look out' of the vehicle while they talk and sing, there is always the prospect that pedestrians or passing drivers will 'look in' as part of the film shoot. Occasionally, guests get out of the SUV, wave to fans from the window or, in the case of Madonna, extend their leg from the vehicle to draw attention to the car as a scene of celebrity filming. While the automobility of 'Carpool Karaoke' is generally hermetic and enclosed, it is public enough to feed curiosity in the scene of famous people being in real cars on actual roads taking a drive.

On occasion, 'Carpool Karaoke' plays with the duality of public and private as part of the drive. Similar to *Comedians in Cars Getting Coffee*, celebrity passengers are not being chauffeured but seen to participate in mundane rituals: from ordering food at a drive-thru to parking up to get a cappuccino. While the audience knows these moments are staged, the situation of the car moves the celebrity beyond formalities of Hollywood where performers and star personas are kept at a distance. Instead, the car provides an up-close environment where the audience is invited to look, overhear and catch celebrities in moments of informality. 'Carpool Karaoke' develops an aesthetic of intimacy loosened by talk, leavened by singing and licensed by the cosy space of automobiles.

The aesthetic of intimacy in 'Carpool Karaoke' reached its apogee in a special episode featuring Michelle Obama in 2016 where the drive takes place in the grounds of the White House. As First Lady at the time, Obama was not a music professional but more than a music star. The episode is simultaneously the least ordinary in circumstance but the most relatable in representing amateur in-car singing. During the 'drive', Obama reveals that

Figure 2.4  In the grounds of the White House, Michelle Obama in 'Carpool Karaoke' (2016)

riding with Corden is only the second time in seven years that she had been able to sit in the passenger seat of a car and listen to music. The pleasures of passengering and 'rocking out' were, in Obama's words, 'a treat'. The fact that Corden's SUV is followed around the grounds of the White House by a secret service vehicle does not spoil the First Lady's evident enjoyment singing hits by Stevie Wonder, Beyoncé and Missy Elliott (who joined in the back of the car to rap a new charity song called 'This Is For My Girls').

Obama's reason for participating in 'Carpool Karaoke' was to promote a government-sponsored educational initiative called 'Let Girls Learn'. Focusing on the education of girls around the world, the objective was to help publicise the launch of the campaign on social media platforms. 'Carpool Karaoke' was ideal for advocacy of this kind given its popularity within and between TV and digital spheres. Beginning with one of Obama's favourite artists, Stevie Wonder ('Signed, Sealed, Delivered I'm Yours'), the selection of karaoke songs would reflect female empowerment, including 'Single Ladies (Put a Ring on It)', 'This Is For My Girls' and 'Get Ur Freak On'. In each case, Obama sings along, raps with accomplishment and gesticulates rhythmically throughout. Discussing media advocacy in a world of online sociality, Stuart

Cunningham and David Craig suggest that 'social media entertainment represents the potential for embracing a progressive cultural politics, even with, and perhaps with the assistance of, its framing within a commercializing environment (2019: 221). In 'hosting' the First Lady, the sonic world of Corden's vehicle became a political platform of its own kind.

Michelle Obama was not the only political luminosity to appear in car-based entertainment in the mid-2010s. President Barack Obama would also feature in an episode of *Comedians in Cars Getting Coffee* towards the end of his second term in office. Six months before the First Lady was driven around the grounds of the White House in the passenger seat of an SUV, the President was picked up by Jerry Seinfeld and driven around the same grounds in the passenger seat of a Corvette Stingray. In December 2015, while the series was still on Crackle, Seinfeld adapted the format of his web show for a politician clearly at ease chatting in a car and having a coffee at a table in the White House canteen. That both online shows gained access to the President and First Lady points to the consecration of the 'drive-and-talk' as a contemporary micro-genre. Reframing 'the vehicle as a performative space of intimate dialogue with the audience', both 'Carpool Karaoke' and *Comedians in Cars Getting Coffee* gained traction in popular culture by playing with the idea of famous people having informal conversation in the space of daily driving. Both shows drew on audience fascination with the scene of passengering, even when driving and talking, motoring and singing, stopped at the perimeter gates of 1600 Pennsylvania Avenue.

## Conclusion: mobile entertainment

Like all 'big things' in the sphere of media entertainment, 'Carpool Karaoke' caught something in the cultural moment. Ventures in short-form streaming were not always successful in the 2010s. Jeffrey Katzenberg's highly capitalised platform Quibi (standing for 'quick bites') was especially short-lived in offering professional entertainment on the go, lasting just six months in 2020.[10] However, 'Carpool Karaoke' managed to maintain itself as a celebrity vehicle. In industrial terms, the segment exemplified the porous borders of television and digital media. It was produced by a major TV network (CBS), born of American late-night television, and delivered through traditional linear broadcasting. 'Carpool Karaoke' won the Primetime Emmy for 'Outstanding Variety Special (pre-recorded)' three times between 2016 and 2019. Crucially, however, 'Carpool Karaoke' also straddled YouTube and was 're-ritualized' within the platform environment.

'Carpool Karaoke' integrated itself into the new screen ecology of social media entertainment by using automobiles as a situation for informal talk and musical performance. Discussing prevalent examples of viral video in the 2010s, including the popular sub-genre of lip-synch videos, Myles McNutt observes that 'the car has been discursively constructed as a space for musical comedy performance for YouTube creators' (2017: 581). The fact that the passengers in 'Carpool Karaoke' were music stars, lip-syncing their own songs, enhanced the sharable nature of the 'drive-and-sing' in this instance. As an example of 'connected viewing' (Holt and Sanson 2014), 'Carpool Karaoke' would demonstrate the attempt by American network television to extend beyond the broadcast environment, in this case bridging late-night TV to the world of online video.

Examining the characteristics of a new kind of broadcasting in the mid-2000s informed by user-generated video, Glen Creeber proposed the term 'web TV' in 2013 to capture developing trends (2013: 126). Considering the 'stripped-down and homemade aesthetic' of online clips, Creeber connects amateur digital video with emergent forms of web TV such as *Lonelygirl 15* (YouTube, 2006–8) and *KateModern* (Bebo, 2007–8). In each case, Creeber notes that online forms produce 'an intensely intimate screen; the most popular images often being those that exploit and understand its power to create a particularly close dynamic between image and audience' (Ibid.: 121). Central to Creeber's analysis is the intimacy of the webcam; he observes that 'its miniature presence (both in camera size and the image it tends to produce) creates a uniquely mediated "private space" that has proven to be immensely popular' (Ibid.: 125). Webcams are associated in his analysis with do-it-yourself videos in the 2000s, often shot in bedrooms. However, the same effect of intimacy might be said of mobile digital cameras in the 2010s; the miniature presence of GoPro devices and similar video technologies helped create the mediated 'private space' of the car in a subsequently popular cultural trend.

Robert Llewellyn's *Carpool* and Jerry Seinfeld's *Comedians in Cars Getting Coffee* were both developed in a moment of experimentation *and* professionalisation in the milieu of 'web TV'. They emerged in the late 2000s and early 2010s when online ventures by TV stars could still feel home-made, or at least unconventional. However, they would crest in a context where YouTube was shifting emphasis from 'user-generated to professional-generated content' and where the online TV industry was coming to the fore (Kim 2012). Catherine Johnson (2019) uses the term 'online TV' to indicate complex industrial interplays between television and digital media in the internet era. She is concerned with the rise of 'closed' online TV services like Netflix, Amazon Prime Video and BBC iPlayer, rather than 'open' platforms such as YouTube, but she points broadly to the 'volatility of television' in a digital media ecosystem that is 'fluid and fast-changing' (2019: 159). Within late-night television's digital turn, 'Carpool Karaoke' can be understood as an attempt in the 2010s to navigate the territories of television and the internet in a moment of significant transition in what TV meant, and continues to mean.

The question that Jerry Seinfeld posed to himself in developing *Comedians in Cars Getting Coffee* – 'what would be a good TV show for a phone?' – also underpins the identity of 'Carpool Karaoke' as mobile entertainment. Simultaneous with the expansion of the online TV industry in the 2010s, the decade was marked by entrepreneurial efforts to create products, apps and services that could occupy consumers during periods of waiting (or killing time) with smartphones and tablets. Ethan Tussey labels this the 'procrastination economy', describing business attempts to 'monetize mobile users' in-between moments' (2018: 6). Tussey conceptualises 'in-between' moments as situations that form part of everyday routines but that are neither work nor leisure as such. They involve transient moments and surroundings such as the commute, the waiting lounge or the office canteen that invite habits of 'media snacking', a widely invoked metaphor for using mobile devices to 'fill downtime' with podcasts, casual games, online videos or social media conversation.

'Carpool Karaoke' is highly suited to the mobile environment that Tussey outlines because it is brief and easy to watch on phones and tablets. Moreover, the conceit *is based* on an 'in-between' moment, namely the commute. Discussing the impact of mobile devices on travel time between work and home, Tussey notes, 'the commute is no longer the epitome of dislocation but rather a site of engagement with friends, family members, and larger cultural conversations' (Ibid.: 74). The nature of this engagement is represented when Corden, as driver, calls his wife from the vehicle and when passengers use their smartphones to connect through Facetime (Stevie Wonder) or send/receive text messages (Jennifer Lopez). 'Carpool Karaoke' assumes an *aesthetic of mobility* on two levels – in the immediate scene of the vehicle in which it is filmed and the way that the 'video vignette' travels between TV and digital contexts. If Corden's ambition with 'Carpool Karaoke' was 'to stay relevant' and 'to be in the conversation', the 'drive-and-sing' not only depicted transitory parts of the day but could also be consumed during these moments.

Across the examples in this book, the habitat of the car is used as a space of intimacy. Glen Creeber makes clear that characteristics of 'intimacy' have defined the small screen aesthetics of television from the early history of the medium. The internet does not represent a new aesthetic regime in this respect but revives and reconstitutes a seemingly authentic 'window on the world' that early media claimed. In this case, the 'drive-and-talk' offered a windscreen on the social, and singing, life of automobiles. *The Trip* series and 'Carpool Karaoke' are alternative content propositions in genre, length and target audience. The former is a contemplative 'comedy of distinction' and the latter an ephemeral 'late-night snack' (Jones 2009: 32). However, they both share concerns with the performance of celebrity in luxury Range Rovers. While 'Carpool Karaoke' is based on the premise of the daily commute, this is used more as a set-up than taken as a real-world reality. In neither *The Trip* nor 'Carpool Karaoke' is the rote experience of being in cars represented. To balance these examples, the final chapter moves away from the focus on celebrities and the signifier of SUVs. Instead, it considers an example of popular comedy entertainment concerned with the everyday experience of commuting and the mundane anthropology of the road, *Peter Kay's Car Share*.

# 3

## *Peter Kay's Car Share*
## On commuting and commonplace roads

In 2014, the BBC launched a new marketing campaign for its iPlayer streaming and download service. Timed to coincide with the Easter vacation, a period when people often take to their cars for the national holiday weekend, the campaign included a series of ten-second promos for iPlayer with the strapline 'download something good before you go'. Appearing in the BBC's regular broadcast schedule, the trailers depicted media viewing beyond conventional, sofa-bound ways of watching TV. Portraying travel delay on motorways, in airports and at ferry ports, the trailers presented iPlayer as suited to the needs of individuals and families on the move, able to distract a nagging child while stuck in traffic or kill time waiting for a car ferry. When iPlayer launched in 2007, the service was portrayed as a luminescent portal that audiences could leap through. By 2014 the promotional impetus changed. Striving to communicate the BBC's role as a digital public service broadcaster, marketing emphasised 'moments and opportunities' where iPlayer could fit into people's daily lives (Grainge 2017). These included moments inside cars.

It was perhaps in-keeping that a year after the 'download something good before you go' campaign, the BBC should use a car-based comedy to experiment with programme release through iPlayer. Following approval by the BBC Trust for a content trial of the Netflix-style model of distributing complete TV seasons at once, the BBC released all six episodes of *Peter Kay's Car Share* on iPlayer before its broadcast launch. A new sitcom based around two characters (John and Kayleigh) making their way to and from work as part of a car share scheme, the series was the first time that original BBC1 content had premiered on iPlayer. The programme was released on iPlayer on 24 April 2015 before being broadcast on BBC1 a week later. The show swiftly broke iPlayer records, becoming the most watched 'box-set' on the service, with 2.8 million views in five days. Far from cannibalising traditional TV viewing, as some feared, the first episode on BBC1 was watched by 6.85 million people, representing 27 per cent of the UK broadcast audience (Conlan 2015). These figures made *Peter Kay's Car Share* (hereafter *Car Share*) one of the highest rated new sitcoms to premiere on any UK channel in the 2010s.

The decision to release *Car Share* on iPlayer was influenced by Peter Kay himself as star, director and co-writer of the series.[1] Although not 'Hollywood' famous like James Corden or Steve Coogan, Kay is one of the most successful live stand-up comedians in the UK with a parallel TV career spanning sitcom, character-based comedy and even guest appearances on the UK's long-running soap opera *Coronation Street* (ITV, 1960–present). *Car Share* was Kay's first work for the BBC and according to Shane Allen, Controller of BBC Comedy, the main reason for distributing the show through iPlayer was 'Peter's trepidation around moving from Channel 4, where he'd done all his work to date, to the much bigger spotlight of BBC1'. Allen elaborates:

> The idea was that premiering the whole series on iPlayer ahead of transmission would act as a soft launch for the series, as he [Kay] wanted people to have the chance to watch more than one episode before making their minds up about it. He hoped people would warm to the core relationship of Kayleigh and John through binge-watching. (cited in Lawson 2018)

We will return to the language of 'binge-watching' at the end of this chapter, a term frequently used in the 2010s to describe contemporary habits of TV viewing. Allen's more immediate point is about Kay moving to BBC1. While the comedian's 'trepidation' about this move is surprising given Kay's widespread popularity (the title *Peter Kay's Car Share* gave the series immediate brand recognition), his previous comedy work in TV involved more niche types of character performance. This ranged from creations such as the wheelchair-using club owner Brian Potter in *Phoenix Nights* (Channel 4, 2001–2) to the gender reassigned reality star Geraldine McQueen in *Peter Kay's Britain's Got the Pop Factor . . . and Possibly a New Celebrity Jesus Christ Soapstar Superstar Strictly on Ice* (Channel 4, 2008). In *Car Share*, Kay plays a naturalistic version of himself in the character of John, a supermarket middle manager who shares his daily commute with Kayleigh, a shop-floor promotions rep played by Sian Gibson.

The series is developed around the simple premise of two co-workers talking in a car about ordinary things while commuting on the highways and byways of Greater Manchester. The success of the first series led to a second series in 2017 made up of just four episodes, with two 'farewell' episodes held back for release in 2018 to complete a twelve-episode run. The farewell episodes include an experimental 'special' where Kay and Gibson improvise conversation in the car, and a 'finale' that brings John and Kayleigh's passengering, and the story of their unfolding romance, to a close. Like other realist sitcoms broadcast on BBC1 in the last two decades, *Car Share* is concerned with the humdrum nature of daily routine and is filmed without a laugh track. Rather than a 'comedy of distinction' like *The Trip* series, *Car Share* represents quotidian British life and belongs to a line of modern sitcoms about the everyday, foregrounding working class characters or encounters within and between white-collar and blue-collar worlds. This is exemplified most notably by *The Royle Family* (BBC2/BBC1, 1998–2012) and *The Office* (BBC2/BBC1, 2001–3).

Writing about *The Royle Family*, Angela Krewani describes the 'extreme reductions' in narrative topic, place and character that distinguish this acclaimed show's presentation of working-class life, seen through the prism of a domestic living room in Manchester and the family ritual of watching TV (2015: 255). *Car Share* is similarly concerned with daily rituals – again, in Greater Manchester – but in the activity of the commute. The programme is based on reductions in topic, place and character created by the situation of the car, in this case focusing on conversations between mid- and lower-level white-collar workers. In narrative terms, each episode uses a two-part structure where John and Kayleigh drive to work (ending in the staff car park before they enter the supermarket) and then drive home (beginning in the staff car park at the end of their shift). The presence of television in *The Royle Family* is substituted in *Car Share* by the ambient sound of local radio. In each episode the fictional station Forever FM ('the fourth biggest station in the North-West') becomes a provider of music, travel bulletins and unintentionally comic advertising inside the vehicle. In imaginative terms, one might think of *Car Share* as poised between the situation of *The Royle Family* and *The Office*; it is concerned with the moment between home and work and what people do and say travelling from one sphere to the other.

*Car Share* appeared a year after *The Trip to Italy* was released on BBC2 and within four weeks of the first airing of 'Carpool Karaoke' on CBS. In the space of twelve months, Coogan, Corden and Kay (a plausible name for a law firm on Forever FM) took the wheel of comedies that became harbingers of experimental TV distribution in the UK and US. In a moment of change for the TV industry, auto-centric entertainments marked the fluid possibilities of film and television (*The Trip*), the porous boundaries of YouTube and network TV ('Carpool Karaoke') and the permeability of digital and broadcast release (*Car Share*). *The Trip* and *Car Share* are similar categories of television; they are both thirty-minute sitcoms commissioned by the BBC that won BAFTA awards for comedy performance. In representational terms, however, *The Trip* and 'Carpool Karaoke' have more in common with each other in the kinds of passengering they depict. Both involve celebrities conversing in big cars in glamorous locales. This compares with *Car Share*, which portrays ordinary characters commuting on commonplace roads.

Rather than fetishize SUVs in sun-kissed backdrops, whether on European road trips or along Sunset Boulevard, *Car Share* explores roads as 'part of our unnoticed collective life' (Moran 2009: 9). The automobile is a quotidian scene in *Car Share*. Perhaps symbolically, the programme departs from the fortress of an expensively upholstered Range Rover and depicts a small red Fiat with a driver-side beady mat. *Car Share* is concerned with the anthropology of the road and approximates the mundane experience of automobility.[2] In critical terms, the programme provides this chapter with a way of thinking about the construction of 'the ordinary' in television comedy.

Kay affectionately described *Car Share* as 'lowest common denominator' (Fane Saunders 2016). Representing nothing more than two supermarket employees brought together by a company car share scheme, Kay's comment deflects the programme's deftness in capturing the comforting banality of the commute and the emotional rapport between the two main characters. In short, it bears out Brett Mills' observation that 'sitcom is a genre which is highly complex but which must pretend it isn't' (2009: 5). The relatability of *Car Share* proved popular with a broad BBC1 audience when the show was released and the series looped back in unforeseen ways in 2020, as I shall examine. In a tumultuous year when ideas of ordinary life were upended by the coronavirus pandemic, *Car Share* became a comedy *for* confinement when Covid-19 put a sudden halt to the commute, in the UK and elsewhere. Made available on iPlayer anew, *Car Share* was suddenly woven into the BBC's public service response to a moment when the emptiness of roads posed questions about normalcy itself and the affinities that people create in the company, and cars, of others.

## *Car Share* and the ordinary

In his cultural history *On Roads*, Joe Moran makes a simple but telling observation about 'ordinary roads'. He writes:

> A road is overlooked and taken for granted because its shared routines seem to offer little opening for individual

creativity or invention. We see most of our journeys on roads as dead time, just a rude interruption of the proper business of living. These everyday roads have penetrated our imaginations obliquely, not through the myth and folklore of the great driving roads but through the compulsive habits and accidental poetry of the commonplace. (2009: 2)

It is fitting that Peter Kay should find the commute a rich vein of comedy, because his act has consistently drawn on the 'accidental poetry of the commonplace'. Coming to prominence in late 1990s as a stand-up comedian, Kay's persona is based around his ordinary, relatable and distinctly Northern identity as an English comic. His live comedy tours have routinely focused on the quirks of everyday behaviour, from the way Dads approach dance floors at discos to the resilience of biscuits when dunking them 'in your brew'. As a mark of Kay's popularity, his *Tour That Doesn't Tour Tour . . . Now on Tour* earned a place in the 2013 edition of *The Guinness World Records* for the most successful stand-up comedy tour of all time, playing to 1.2 million people in 113 arenas across the UK.

Kay's stand-up career has developed in parallel with roles in popular TV comedy, writing and starring in the spoof documentary series *That Peter Kay Thing* (Channel 4, 2000), sitcoms such as *Phoenix Nights* and its spin-off *Max and Paddy's Road to Nowhere* (Channel 4, 2004) and a satire of TV talent formats, *Peter Kay's Britain's Got the Pop Factor*. Between wry caricatures of British life, Kay's comedy persona was amplified in the 2000s by charity skits for BBC Comic Relief, reprising the Tony Christie song 'Amarillo' and a cabaret version of The Proclaimers' 'I'm Gonna Be (500 Miles)' with a roster of former light entertainment celebrities. He also appeared in humorous TV ads for John Smith's bitter, personifying the strapline of Northern 'no nonsense'.[3] As a fixture of British entertainment culture since 2000, Kay has developed an unpretentious, everyman style of comedy worked over in different formats. The inclusion of his name in TV titles such as *Peter Kay's Britain's Got the Pop Factor* and *Peter Kay's Car Share* has become a shorthand in UK television for shows with populist comedy appeal.

Warm, nostalgic and frequently drawing on material from his upbringing and jobs in the English town of Bolton (including stints at a bingo hall and a supermarket), a fellow comedian remarked that British audiences feel that Kay 'belongs to us' (Dolan 2019).[4] Of course, the 'us' in this statement begs the question 'which us'? To answer, I would borrow from Andy Medhurst's (2007) enjoyable book on popular TV comedy and English cultural identities, *A National Joke*. While the concept of the national is slippery, involving complex intersections of class, gender, ethnicity, age, region and so on, Medhurst playfully argues that 'English comedy widely acclaimed by English audiences contributes significantly to how English culture has imagined its Englishness' (Ibid.: 1). In the same way that Alan Bennett or Victoria Wood are sometimes called 'national treasures' for the way they anatomise England in their comedy writing and characters, Peter Kay is part of a tradition of British-cum-English performers whose Northern-inflected comedy is built around observing the ordinary. This tradition relies less on arch irony or the creation of grotesques than 'social comedy and vignettes of everyday life' (Hogan 2017a: 34).

There is little more ordinary than roads, especially when these 'meld into mundane life, vanish into unnoticed routine' (Moran 2009: 16). Kay's first significant TV project, in 1998, was inspired by the mundane nature of roads in a standalone episode for Channel 4's *Comedy Lab* strand (1998–2005) called 'The Services'.[5] Functioning as a pilot for *That Peter Kay Thing*, 'The Services' followed different characters in a motorway service station, many played by Kay but also featuring Sian Gibson, his college friend and future collaborator on *Car Share*. The choice of a service station was typical of Kay's eye for comedy of the commonplace. Joe Moran dedicates an entire chapter to the history of motorway service stations in *On Roads*. He points out that while service stations are unceremonious features of the roadside, 'non-places' that people use fleetingly and distractedly, they are nevertheless part of the collective experience of motorway travel, spaces that have their 'own rhythms and cadences, their own interior lives' (2009: 160). Foreshadowing elements that would feature in *Car Share*, one character in 'The Services' is a mobile DJ who sets up turntables in the forlorn car park of the service station to play 1980s records, part of a bid to help Chorley FM secure an FM licence. Nearly two decades later, Chorley FM would be reborn as Forever FM and Kay would turn his attention to the habitat of the car rather than the interior life of Bolton services.

The concept of the ordinary has been taken up in various ways within television studies. Frances Bonner uses the term 'ordinary television' to describe programmes like TV game shows, lifestyle formats, daytime chat shows, advice programmes and other non-fiction genres that involve the 'direct address of the audience, the incorporation of ordinary people into the programme and the mundanity of [their] concerns' (2003: 3). Terms like 'ordinary' and 'mundanity' are not used disparagingly here but are instead taken up to examine (and treat seriously) TV's representation of the everyday, quotidian, familiar and routine. Ordinary television is constituted in opposition to 'special television' in Bonner's account. *Car Share* would be an example of special television by her definition; it was widely promoted fictional television garlanded with major TV awards, winning the BAFTA for Best Male Comedy Performance and Best Scripted Comedy in 2016. Similar to *The Royle Family* and *The Office*, both of which 'aspired to an unusually high level of naturalistic credibility' (Walters 2005: 23), *Car Share* constructs the ordinary through particular narrative conventions, staging decisions, camera shots and performance styles. However, each show is explicitly concerned with the mundane, portraying characters and routines that are unexceptional and ordinary at the level of popular identification.

The observational comedy in *Car Share* encourages TV audiences to see parallels between on-screen representations and their own lived experience. Specifically, it invites recognition of the lived experience of the commute. The 2011 UK census revealed that 59 per cent of the British population travelled to work each day either by driving or getting a lift in a car or van. Statistically,

**Figure 3.1** John's Fiat and the anthropology of the road, *Car Share* (2015)

the average worker spent 54 minutes commuting each day in the early 2010s, the average driver spending the equivalent of 4.5 working weeks on roads (Roxby 2014). Focusing on journeys in the morning and afternoon rush hour, *Car Share* has a circular episodic pattern that takes account of the repetitive nature of commuting. In driving to and from work, the situation of the comedy is in the car but also *on the road*. Unlike 'Carpool Karaoke', where the drive is secondary to the performance of songs inside a tinted SUV, attention is given to the sights and sounds of the commute: from the choreography of traffic on ring-roads, roundabouts and commercial high-streets to the sound of traffic bulletins with their litany of stock expressions about tailbacks. Shots of John's Fiat 500 are intercut with scenes that convey a broad sense of urban commuting and of people making their way between home and work. Just as *The Office* lingers on intercuts of plants, photocopiers and workplace objects in each episode, *Car Share* is interspersed with scenes of trams, buses, cycle lanes, pedestrians, even a canal boat.

The relatability of the road in *Car Share* is not dependent on recognising the experience of the commute in Greater Manchester but on the general anthropology of the scene. This said, I often found myself leaning in to see if I recognised the route of the journey based on my occasional visits to Manchester. One friend did, in fact, spot John's car passing the end of his childhood street in one episode. However, the frames before and after were in a different neighbourhood entirely, suggesting a constructed visual grammar of the road within and between episodes.[6] The locations of *Car Share* range across Bury, Burnley, Wirral and Southport, but are mainly in and around Manchester, Bolton, Altrincham and Salford. While set in the North of England, *Car Share* features common sights of the urban and commuting environment in the UK, and these become part of the quotidian landscape. In Greater Manchester, as would be found in Bristol, Birmingham, Norwich or Brighton, the journey to work takes in fast-food outlets and betting shop chains, the passing font of traffic signs, the composition of crossings, verges, roundabouts and junctions and the street architecture of bus stops and billboards.

Roadside billboards are a source of cutaway sight gags throughout *Car Share*. The constructed visual grammar of the road extends to a literal grammar of gags that must be spotted, from 'Brazilian wax while you wait' to 'one meal for the price of two'. In an episode that involves John and Kayleigh taking a 'sickie' and going on a day trip to Wigan, multiple sight gags play on the town's real-life association with pies ('Cash4Pies', 'pies sale now on', 'no pies left in this van overnight'). These sight gags are accompanied by local radio advertising within the car. In the show's comic exploration of the repetitive, Forever FM plays the same ads recurrently so that audiences become familiar with local butchers, shed suppliers and education providers like 'Brillington College – where brilliant is almost our name'. *Car Share* is a portrait of what it means to occupy a vehicle on mundane journeys; it explores the habitat of the car but also the habitual nature of the road and the familiarity of driving the same route at ritual times of the day.

The road becomes fodder for conversation between John and Kayleigh in this context. The sitcom departs from *The Trip* and 'Carpool Karaoke' on these terms. In considering the social dimension of being in cars, the series explores different facets of human behaviour among the micro-society of motorists, passengers and rides in general. On their second journey together, Kayleigh states matter-of-factly that she went dogging the previous day with her 80-year-old neighbour Ken. This invites a lengthy debate about the meaning of dogging, Kayleigh insisting that the word refers to dog-walking and John countering that it refers to the practice of having sex in a car with people watching. This sets up a back and forth between the two, Kayleigh standing her ground, John astonished and amused at Kayleigh's misapprehension, guffawing at the idea that she owns a bumper sticker that reads 'dogging's for life, not just for Christmas'. The debate is resolved by pulling up to a curb and Kayleigh asking a passing male dog-walker to settle the definition, an exchange where the question and response are heard differently until the pedestrian conspiratorially affirms the 'joys of dogging' in no uncertain terms.

While dogging is perhaps an extreme example of the duality of the car as private and public space, *Car Share* plays with the simultaneously private and public nature of vehicles on roads. *Car Share* is about passengering but extends to interactions with pedestrians, cyclists and other drivers in moments when the vehicle has stopped at traffic lights or junctions. The observational comedy draws on familiar situations of the road: flirting with adjacent drivers, being caught singing unawares, passing co-workers waiting at a bus stop. Scenes take place in a petrol station, car wash, drive-thru and even a safari park when John and Kayleigh go on their day trip to Wigan. The naturalism of *Car Share* does not preclude moments of pantomime. Following their visit to the safari park, John and Kayleigh discover they have a monkey on the roof and end up literally driving in circles to send the chimp to sleep in the back seat, John declaring 'I can't believe this is happening, it's like a shit comedy'. Unlike *The Office*, where any scene that appeared wacky or farcical was cut, the naturalism of *Car Share* is punctuated by slapstick and nods to traditional sitcom.[7] This ranges from Kayleigh inadvertently squirting a sample of urine over John when she rams a plastic bottle into the vehicle's cup holder, to an entire episode where John, Kayleigh and a fellow employee drive to an evening work party dressed as Harry Potter, Hagrid and a Smurf.

**Figure 3.2** The incredulity of drivers, *Car Share* (2017)

Interactions with people outside the car provide a way of dramatising behaviours of the road. In a study of annoyed motorists in Los Angeles, the ethnographer Jack Katz notes the 'routine production of a sense of incredulity' among drivers in LA around minor transgressions like tailgating or horn-honking (1999: 28). In representing the culture of the road, *Car Share* includes altercations and conveys John's incredulity in several different situations. Emboldened by the private space of his car, he rails at a workman who crosses the road in front of a school lollipop lady and he argues with a cyclist who rests a drink on the roof of his Fiat while waiting at traffic lights. If 'the road creates its own mentalities and delusions, its own ways of relating to others' (Moran 2009: 121), *Car Share* uses the road as a context for the mild ennui that Brett Mills suggests has been at the core of British sitcom since its inception (Mills 2015: 272).

The confinement of the car has been used previously in 'Britcom' featuring characters renowned for their ennui. As Mills points out, the traditional sitcom *One Foot in the Grave* (BBC1, 1990–2000), focusing on the curmudgeonly retiree Victor Meldrew, set a number of episodes in a single location. This included 'The Beast in the Cage' (1993) where Victor, his wife and their friend Mrs Warboys find themselves trapped in a motorway traffic jam. Victor's incessant moaning about the crawling traffic, the faulty elements of his car, the distraction of snacks and the behaviour of other motorists is mirrored in John's periodic frustration at the behaviour of pedestrians, cyclists and other drivers. Sitting in gridlocked unison with other cars is a common British motoring experience and there are many different codes of behaviour in these, and other, moments of everyday automobility. Using the situation of the commute, *Car Share* draws on the complex ecology of driving to find humour on highways, laughs in laybys, mirth in routine mobility.

As mentioned, the sitcom features a small runabout vehicle rather than a statement SUV. However, John's engagement with the technological features of the automobile is more pronounced than 'Coogan' or Corden in their luxury Range Rovers. In an article called 'Driving in the City', inspired by Michel De Certeau's work on the practice of everyday life, Nigel Thrift (2004) reflects on the nature of contemporary driving. Pointedly, he notes that only since the 1990s has computer software become an integral element of mass market automobiles. The manifestations of this software extend to engine management, brakes, suspension, parking and security, but also to entertainment and communication systems. The modern car has become a software platform, among other things, and *Car Share* captures the driver's relationship with digital gadgetry as part of the twenty-first-century commute. The first series, for example, opens with John arguing with his softly spoken sat-nav, exasperated when he is sent down cul-de-sacs ('you're off your tits') and personifying his relationship with the female voice ('me and you are going to fall out'). *Car Share* also represents John's use of the car speakerphone, his character occasionally pressing a button on the steering wheel to enable conversation in the car. This allows the sitcom to extend who is 'inside' and 'outside' the car in a narrative and spatial sense. The speakerphone enables John and Kayleigh to commute separately together in certain instances (John in his car, Kayleigh on the metro or bus) and becomes a way for off-screen characters to enter the audio space of the car, setting up comic situations where

Kayleigh hears herself discussed, pejoratively, by one of John's fellow managers.

The construction of the ordinary is not simply about mundane situations and routines. It also involves the depiction of everyday people and relationships. *Car Share* is a sitcom about the road but also a romance within a car. In their ethnographic study of commuting, Eric Laurier and Hayden Lorimer suggest that car sharing is like a form of co-habitation, writing:

> those who share cars to commute become acquaintances of a special kind, in some ways akin to people sharing a flat. Unsurprisingly, people who car share can become friends, come to detest one another or, as some of our participants reported, it can lead to romance. Car-sharers have in common the qualities of regular contact, a certain inescapable intimacy and their duration. (2012: 211)

John and Kayleigh develop friendship and courtship through the 'inescapable intimacy' of their daily commute. This is fostered in conversations about dating, music, past relationships, life hopes, singledom, work gossip, thwarted ambitions and memories of growing up. 'I tell you more than anyone else', Kayleigh reflects at one point, to which John replies philosophically, 'well, that's car sharing for you'.

*Car Share* is an automotive 'will-they-won't-they' romance. The representation of a male driver and a female passenger underscores the conventional, heteronormative depiction of gender roles and relations in this context.[8] John is emotionally guarded and finds it difficult to share his feelings in the car, while Kayleigh is open, admits to her romantic hopes and is willing to confide that 'all I've ever wanted is to meet the man of my dreams and have babies'. The arrangements of passengering in the sitcom underlie traditional inscriptions of male and female identity. Notably, the car belongs to John and he acts as 'host' to Kayleigh in the protocol of car sharing. Kayleigh does take the wheel of the Fiat after John sprains his arm in a misjudged dash to post a letter while queuing in traffic. However, John cannot resist remarking on her 'female' driving style ('come on Miss Daisy, put your foot down') and the episode concludes with the car breaking down, transpiring that Kayleigh has inadvertently filled up the Fiat with petrol rather than the required diesel.

The confinement of the car deters John from sharing his hopes and thoughts of courting, at least directly. It is perhaps no coincidence, given John's emotional inarticulacy within the vehicle, that the pair manage their first cuddle on public transport. Following an accident where a passing lorry rips off John's car door (after the nurturing Kayleigh insists on rescuing a hedgehog in the road), the pair are no longer exclusively in John's space and the series ends with the two 'car share buddies' holding hands on the back seat of a bus. Describing the unsettling nature of road accidents, Joe Moran suggests that 'suddenly, the everyday stops being invisible and the road is no longer about the endless movement of traffic. For a brief moment, the smooth continuum of daily life, the illusion that it has no past or future, has been broken like a spell' (2009: 195). Rendered speechless by his near-death mishap, there is a certain spell-breaking in the gender arrangements following John's car being towed. The sitcom is resolved in heterosexual harmony but with John occupying the right-hand 'passenger' position on the bus and Kayleigh taking control of the romantic gears.

While *Car Share* is conventional in its construction of 'ordinary' gender relationships, the sitcom resists simple cliché. Brett Mills and Mark Rimmer note that one of Kayleigh's first acts in the car is to switch the radio station from the male-centred BBC Radio 5Live (a real talk radio station focused on sport) to Forever FM, a station whose musical content and jingles orient towards a female listenership. Reading *Car Share* through the sitcom's use of popular music, Mills and Rimmer suggest that 'Kayleigh's first meaningful gesture is to feminise the car's auditory space' (2017: 176). The sitcom denotes subtle interplays of gender, as well as workplace relations, through such acts. The relationship between management and shopfloor workers is a staple of British sitcom, from programmes such as *Rag Trade* (BBC1, 1962–63) to more recent series like *The Office* and the supermarket-based *Trollied* (Sky1, 2011–18). Male management culture is actively lampooned in *Car Share* when it intrudes in the vehicle. Kayleigh is especially contemptuous of John's slippage into 'the jive' of business speak, for example, when he talks on the car speakerphone of 'pushing the envelope' and 'dealing with a curveball'. While passengering in *Car Share* embodies hierarchies of gender and work – between men and women, management and shopfloor staff – the series uses the interior space of the car to complicate certainties of emotional and professional identity. For John and Kayleigh, passengering becomes a conduit for connection; the automobile is a space of affinity in *Car Share*, as well as a vehicle for occasional transports of fantasy. As I explore in the next section, the sense of connection between the main characters is often catalysed by the ambient companion of car radio.

## Affinity and daydreaming in the space of the car

The sociologist Jennifer Mason uses the example of 'driving and thinking' to consider *what* we see, encounter and experience in the activity of driving and *how* we feel, emote and dream in the process of doing it. Her project is to consider feelings of affinity in social life as these relate to people, place, movement and environment, taking account of what she calls the 'socio-atmospherics of everyday life' (2018: 123–5). In her unconventional study, Mason characterises affinities as 'encounters where it is possible to identify a spark or charge of connection that makes personal life charismatic, or enchants, or even toxifies it' (Ibid.: 1). *Car Share* provides a portrait of spark and charge in the environment of the car. I would argue that part of the pleasure of the sitcom is the way it turns the 'atmospherics' of the daily commute into something charismatic.

Mason suggests that affinities come alive in sensations, their potency coming 'from the frissons, charges, alluring discordances and poetics that animate and enliven everyday personal lives' (2018: 200). In *Car Share*, these sensations and frissons frequently stem from music on the car radio, returning focus to the sonic world of the automobile introduced in Chapter 2. Peter Kay referred to the car radio as 'a strong third character' in *Car Share* (Jefferies 2015). Forever FM provides a stream of traffic bulletins, quizzes and local advertising but also a playlist of pop songs assiduously drawn from the 1980s and 1990s (motto, 'timeless hits now and forever'). The sitcom taps into nostalgia for these decades in various ways: through conversational references to Woolworths and Wimpy, cassettes and crimpers, but most immediately through chart music. The sound of fondly remembered hits from the eighties and nineties provides a soundtrack in each episode. Sometimes, lyrics mirror feelings in the car – 'Turn Back the Clock', 'Love Changes Everything', 'Ordinary World', 'I Believe in You' – and at other times songs create mood for a time of day, Forever FM playing romantic ballads when John takes Kayleigh and a drunk colleague home after a late-night work party (motto, 'timeless songs, timeless love').

For Brett Mills and Mark Rimmer, the radio station is 'not merely background noise intended to signify a realist depiction; it is integral to the functioning of the comedy and the depiction of the characters' (2017: 172). Similar to 'Carpool Karaoke', John and Kayleigh find themselves singing along to pop music in the vehicle and these moments become a basis for affinity. Mills and Rimmer note that popular music becomes a catalyst for John's self-sufficient exterior to soften, his enjoyment of distantly remembered chart hits gradually cementing his connection with Kayleigh. Music is key to the 'atmospherics' of the car. It provides the programme's soundtrack and functions at a diegetic level where the characters listen to, comment on and engage with the music directly. However, pop songs also give rise to sporadic daydreams during the commute. These are experienced mostly by Kayleigh as passenger, transforming automotive window-gazing into flights of imagination.

The dream sequences are discordant moments in the sitcom's naturalistic depiction of driving and passengering. As fantasies,

**Figure 3.3** Daydreaming during the commute, 'Rush Hour' in *Car Share* (2017)

they depict Kayleigh or John, in costume, reconstructing music videos inspired by a song playing on Forever FM. These daydreams include MTV-style renditions of Anastasia ('I'm Outta Love'), Cyndi Lauper ('True Colors'), Cliff Richard ('Devil Woman') and Take That ('Back for Good'). Other sequences develop from Kayleigh's fertile imagination, including a personalised cartoon of 'The Beautiful Briny Sea' from *Bedknobs and Broomsticks* (1971) that she urgently conjures to help deal with a panic attack in a car wash. Two daydreams are linked to the romantic storyline of the series. In the final episode of Series 1, Kayleigh imagines herself driving with John in an amorous Kodachrome rendering of Jane Wiedlin's 'Rush Hour'.

More poignantly, the final episode of Series 2 finds John imagining a grand romantic gesture that he has, in fact, botched in real life. In this case, 'music video John' climbs over cars stuck in traffic to reach his sweetheart riding in a taxi ahead. While the sequence plays out to Marillion's 'Kayleigh', it parodies the music video of REM's 'Everybody Hurts' (1992) where the interior thoughts of people in cars, stuck on a highway, are written on-screen before people collectively abandon their vehicles and emotional confinements. In the music video fantasy, John ends by kissing Kayleigh in a swooning dip. This disguises the reality of John being stuck in traffic after Kayleigh abandons the car, frustrated at John's inability to admit his feelings ('I'm getting out of your car, out of your life', she exclaims). The series ends with John's thwarted attempt to express himself through a dedication to Kayleigh on Forever FM.

These dream sequences remove the audience from the 'reality' of the commute. They are incongruous moments but they approximate something familiar in the activity of passengering – letting the mind wander. Jennifer Mason reflects on 'the filaments of affinity' produced by in-car music, a sensory experience that can heighten the emotional climate within a vehicle but also project outwards onto the passing landscape (2018: 145–6). While the selection of in-car music will differ for individual drivers, Mason points to music's capacity to stir feelings and personal memories. In *Car Share*, music becomes a source of nostalgia but also leads to transports of imagination, enabling subtleties of character and subtexts of romance to emerge.

Mills and Rimmer argue that music in *Car Share* 'is both resolutely ordinary and highly meaningful, and over the series John learns to appreciate and vocalise what this music might, and does, mean for him' (2017: 172). In constructing 'ordinary' taste, they suggest that the programme celebrates music that is often maligned. This is symbolised by Kayleigh giving John a copy of the pop compilation 'Now That's What I Call Music 48' at the end of Series 1, principally to convey her feelings through the lyrics of a Hear'Say hit. Although John is sceptical of a song by a group of reality talent show winners ('load of shite') and incredulous that her favourite album *could be* 'Now 48', John grins when he realises the romantic intent. The first series concludes with John driving and singing along to 'Pure and Simple', buoyed by the chorus line, 'wherever you go . . . whatever you do . . . it's pure and simple . . . I'll be there for you'. The combination of music and motoring turns the habitat of the car into a space of enchantment. In another moment in Series 2, John and Kayleigh instinctively hold hands to sing the chorus of Billy Ocean's 'Red Light Spells

**Figure 3.4** The exuberance of singing in cars, *Car Share* (2017)

Danger'. Expressing his joy, John exclaims, 'I love this! . . . us . . . driving . . . singing!'. As Mills and Rimmer note, music in such moments enables the main characters to signal what might otherwise go unexpressed.

Forever FM becomes the spur of passengering in *Car Share*; radio acts as a catalyst for what Lucy Fife Donaldson and James Walters call 'patterns of expressive rapport' (2018: 358). Examining TV acting in confined space, especially car interiors, Donaldson and Walters consider how environmental elements place 'specific demands on actors to maintain basic rudiments of behaviour while, at the same time, providing occasions to infuse their actions and reactions with detailed layers of meaning and significance' (2018: 357). They elaborate:

> [B]ecause car journeys have an innately practical or even mundane purpose, there is a creative pressure in finding points of dramatic interest in cars, which in turn places a responsibility upon performers to help make the car interior an engaging space. The tension of balancing public and private behaviours, and how these are to be negotiated, is further intensified in a space that is physically contained while also being on display to the outside world. (Ibid.: 358)

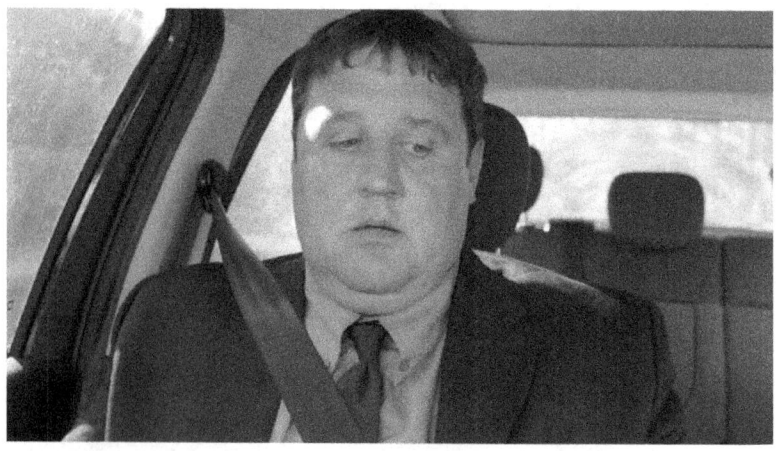

**Figure 3.5** Glancing at Forever FM, *Car Share* (2015)

In terms of performance, the car radio provides a point of focus in *Car Share* that turns the vehicle into 'an engaging space'. Donaldson and Walters note that, within cars, 'fixed seating positions, low ceiling heights and narrow internal widths can all curtail opportunities for the performance of elaborate or complex movements or gestures' (Ibid.: 358). Car-based scenes often rely on discreet details of acting in this context. In *Car Share*, the camera dwells on facial expressions, including subtle glances that become ways of conveying meaning, from John's incredulity at the way Kayleigh feigns a sickie to their mutual amusement at a 'radio balls up' on Forever FM. The situation of driving means that John's character needs to be plausibly engaged with 'watching the road'. Shot with camera set-ups that follow the direction of speech inside the vehicle, including close-up reaction shots to comments made in person or on the radio, *Car Share* frequently dwells on John's glances. These are layered with expressive meaning, whether shocked at Kayleigh's misapprehension at the word 'dogging' or quizzical when he hears something unintended (or pun-intended) on local radio advertising ('Give your mouth a treat, try Ken's meat').

Just as *The Trip* uses meandering car journeys to enact middle-aged melancholy, there is a similar sense of life reflection in *Car*

*Share*'s short, but repeated, commutes to work. Between John's world-weariness and Kayleigh's anxiety about life passing her by, the car becomes a space for taking stock. In the arc of the series, however, John's defensive attitude to relationships ('bollocks to love') and Kayleigh's dashed hopes for dating are replaced by growing rapport between the pair. The repetition of commuting helps disclose intricacies of character that lead to feelings of affinity between driver and passenger, culminating in romance.

In narrative terms, the 'will-they-won't-they' storyline became a source of national TV interest, as well as fan petitioning.[9] Bearing out the mainstream popularity of the series, the viewing figures for the finale, broadcast on BBC1 in May 2018, peaked at 6.4m viewers, which represented 34.2 per cent of the broadcast audience. The culmination of the series was received enthusiastically. The TV critic Mark Lawson went as far as to write that *Car Share* 'will stand as one of the highest achievements of twenty-first century TV comedy, containing a combination of warmth and cleverness, social observation and romance, originality and nods to TV comedy history that only Kay could achieve' (Lawson 2018). With this level of popular appeal and comedy acclaim, it was perhaps no surprise that the BBC would reprise the series in the crisis year of 2020. In the final section, I consider the cultural resonance of *Car Share* as it was positioned to meet very particular social and audience needs.

## Comedy for confinement in the time of Covid-19

In normal circumstances, roads are overlooked and taken for granted. The same might be said of our social life in cars, including the experience of giving people a lift and sharing a ride. The global pandemic caused by the Covid-19 virus halted people's everyday use of roads for a brief, but profound, moment of time. The UK entered a period of national lockdown on 23 March 2020 following the British Prime Minister, Boris Johnson, announcing that people must stay at home. Together with the closure of many 'non-essential' shops and businesses, The Coronavirus Act, which came into force on 25 March, gave government departments the power to shut schools and nurseries. The result was a virtual emptying of streets and highways; the rhythms and habits of the road were suspended for months as cars were used only occasionally by the majority, mostly for brief shopping forays. The novelist Zadie Smith described the pandemic as a 'global humbling' (2020: 6). A feature of this humbling was a re-evaluation of norms. This included everyday practices like driving that people were suddenly forced to 'see' because they could no longer do them in the same way.

In the first weeks of lockdown, the effects of the coronavirus pandemic on the car industry were discussed as a bell-weather. The UK car market was widely reported in the national press as having 'ground to a halt' in April 2020, vehicle sales plummeting by 97 per cent to the lowest level since the end of World War Two. In the same period, road traffic in the UK fell to levels not seen since 1955 (Jolly 2020). While the economic impact of lockdown on the car industry was stark, the effect on carbon emissions seemed portentous and experiments in reclaiming the streets appeared to signal a recalibration of people's relation with roads. Opinion pieces began to invite people to 'imagine an end to our long love affair with cars' (Rustin 2020). The effect and legacy of the pandemic will be written in history and it is not my intention to analyse the impact of lockdown on automobility. However, I am interested in the way that television programmes were used during the UK lockdown to respond to the purported needs of TV audiences, specifically how *Car Share* tapped nostalgia of an immediate kind.

On 10 April 2020, several weeks into the first UK lockdown, Peter Kay released a new audio-only episode of *Car Share* on iPlayer. Quickly written by Kay, Sian Gibson and Paul Coleman, the episode lasted twenty minutes and was, in Kay's words, a purposeful 'effort to try to cheer people up' (Craig 2020).[10] Restrictions on social distancing meant that television could not be filmed in a car; like millions of people in the UK it was no longer possible for a driver and passenger to be together in a vehicle unless with members of their own family. The suspension of TV production across a roster of genres meant that a show entirely based in a car, filmed on roads and set during a busy commute was triply unfeasible. Kay commented: 'obviously we weren't able to film anything because of the lockdown but I hope people will use their imagination and enjoy listening . . . here's hoping people enjoy having John and Kayleigh back. Lord knows we need it right now' (Ibid.). Released on Good Friday, the audio episode would include spoof ads and weather reports, and featured John and Kayleigh sharing memories from the 1980s (BMXs, body popping, teenage sexual fumblings) and singing along to upbeat pop music on Forever FM (John Paul Young's 'Love is in The Air', S Club 7's 'Reach for the Stars').

The audio episode appeared on iPlayer for nineteen days, after which the BBC aired the whole of *Car Share* again on BBC1. The 'box-set' of all twelve episodes was also made available on iPlayer for five months. As people were confined to their homes during waves of lockdown during 2020, television viewing rocketed. In the first three weeks of lockdown across March and April, the BBC saw viewing figures increase by 23 per cent, with more than a third of all television viewing in the UK streamed and channelled through the BBC (Johnson 2020a). This gave renewed vigour to the BBC's public service identity. Before the coronavirus pandemic, and for much of the 2010s, the BBC faced attack from hostile commercial rivals and a Conservative government intent on reducing its size. Several months after the initial release of *Car Share* in 2015, for example, the government's Culture Secretary, John Whittingdale, published a green paper with proposals designed to narrow the BBC's scope. This included the suggestion that the Corporation no longer make popular entertainment but, instead, restrict itself to highbrow programming supplied less readily by commercial broadcasters. As a post-election broadside, this was timed to coincide with the review of the BBC's charter in 2016. The original launch of *Car Share* can be set against a background of politicised discussion about the role of the BBC, including government proposals to reduce the provision of shared viewing experiences around popular entertainment.

While detractors of the BBC continued to use the Corporation as a punch bag, the pandemic offered a clear lesson in the value of public service media. In May 2020, the creative and broadcast design agency Red Bee Media circulated a report titled 'Audiences in lockdown: how Covid-19 has supercharged the power of TV'. This posed a fundamental question for TV and media practitioners: 'how are audience needs evolving during the different stages of the human response to the pandemic? And how are broadcasters responding?' Directly alluding to the BBC, the report suggested that 'TV's power to inform, entertain, educate and unite has rarely been so important' (Red Bee Media 2020: 2). It went on to propose '12 observations based on audience needs', from the function of television to provide 'clarity (navigating the infodemic)' and 'perspective (exploring our cultural identity)' to the offer of 'comfort (the warm bath of nostalgia)' and 'belonging (all together now)'.

The observational comedy of *Car Share* was squarely in the spectrum of comfort. Focusing on ordinary people sharing everyday routines, the representation of the commute offered nostalgia for life before lockdown. Shane Allen, Controller of BBC Comedy, would comment in April 2020, '*Car Share* was one of the major comedy hits of the last decade and is just the tonic for our times' (Gillibrand 2020). As a mainstream BBC1 show, the sitcom transitioned from a comedy *of* confinement to a comedy *for* confinement. The depiction of two people sharing the space of a car became a poignant reminder of social behaviour curtailed, of human interaction before the hiatus.

*Car Share* symbolised the ability of public service media to draw on assets (programmes, distribution platforms) to serve pressing cultural purposes. The behavioural language of 'needstates' became part of BBC management vernacular in the 2010s and iPlayer, the original launch vehicle of *Car Share*, was central to the Corporation's strategic thinking (Grainge and Johnson 2018).

In 2012, the Head of TV Content for BBC iPlayer, Victoria Jaye, commented that rather than simply present audiences with new, clever technology, iPlayer had 'to answer a need for [audiences] ... we have got to solve their entertainment needs' (Victoria Jaye, cited in Grainge 2017: 9). The coronavirus pandemic threw the notion of 'needs' into new and dramatic relief. As the expression of the BBC online, iPlayer became a digital means to inform, educate and entertain during lockdown. Catherine Johnson cautions that it is important not to assume that everybody has the technological facility and cultural skills necessary to access digital television (2020a). However, for many in 2020, iPlayer provided a vital source of news, educational support, comedy and arts programming, including bespoke forms of BBC content such as the Corporation's 'Culture in Quarantine' strand.[11]

*Car Share* was just one part of the BBC's attempt to tailor its mix of lockdown programming. The sitcom was part of a diet of content designed to meet the needs – both practical and psychological – of a housebound population. According to data records of programmes available on iPlayer between March and August 2020, extracted and examined by the TV studies academic J. P. Kelly, 'comedy' was the dominant primetime genre on the service during lockdown (4090 records), followed by 'drama' (3947), 'film' (2316) and 'documentary and documentary film' (2181) (Kelly 2021).[12] Kelly conducted a macroscopic analysis of BBC iPlayer between August 2018 and August 2020, a period that included the first phase of the national UK lockdown. Over two years, Kelly 'web-scraped' the iPlayer interface once a day between the hours of 8pm and 11pm, providing data that enabled him to track patterns in the prevalence and positioning of content on the service. As part of his 'distant reading' of iPlayer in the late 2010s, Kelly notes the increasing number of box-sets made available by the BBC, referring to an entire series or multiple seasons of a particular show. While the availability of box-sets peaked each December during his study, comprising 50 per cent of the iPlayer interface (correlating with the Christmas period), his data shows a spike in box-set availability from March 2020. Significantly, *comedy box-sets* became a prominent part of the BBC's content mix during the first months of the coronavirus outbreak.

Kelly's research contributes to debates about 'content prioritisation' on video-on-demand (VOD) services. This is an emerging concern in TV studies and draws attention to the types of programme that are made prominent and discoverable through online interfaces compared with those which are less obvious and harder to find. Kelly extracted *Car Share* from his data to provide me with a picture of the programme's availability on iPlayer since 2018, including the show's literal position on the landing screen over time. While there were no records of the programme on iPlayer in 2018 and 2019, the box-set (featuring all twelve episodes) appeared in the data-set from May 2020. Although *Car Share* was the first original BBC1 programme to be released on iPlayer as a box-set in 2015, therefore, the series was made unavailable after its initial broadcast run. It would take two years for the show to appear again on iPlayer. At this point, *Car Share* assumed a reasonably prominent position on the service. The generic (which is to say non-personalised) version of iPlayer has a landing screen organised with twelve horizontal programme tiles in ten vertical rows, with users able to navigate up, down, left and right. In browsing for content, the most visible, and discoverable, position for a programme is the first row and first column. Between May and September 2020, *Car Share* appeared regularly in columns 1–3 (36 times) and most frequently in row 6 (55 times). It appeared in the first row 31 times.[13] The broader point, in this kind of analysis, is the role that VOD interfaces play in shaping content recommendations.

Focusing on the growth of TV apps in the mid-late 2010s, Catherine Johnson argues that there is 'an economics of prominence' at work in the way that programmes and movies are made discoverable by commercial VOD platforms like Netflix, Amazon Prime Video and Apple TV. She notes that the growing ecology of TV apps presents questions for public service media, specifically how to maintain public value in a media market dominated by platforms that operate through 'datafication, commodification and selection' (Johnson 2020b: 178). As a VOD service, BBC iPlayer can be accessed as an app on smartphones, tablets, smart TVs, digital media players and games consoles. Rather than rely on data-driven personalisation, however, iPlayer has paired algorithmic approaches to content recommendation with editorially 'curated' journeys between different kinds of TV. In public service terms, the BBC has sought to maintain an ethos of 'serendipitous discovery' through digital as well as broadcast channels, encouraging variety in invitations to view. While box-sets arguably temper this ethos, inviting 'more-of-the-same', the prominence of *Car Share* on iPlayer substantiated the BBC's claim that its on-demand service is a 'cutting edge tech platform – but it's run by humans. Not assembled by algorithm, but carefully curated by people' (Moore 2019). Making the show available on iPlayer during lockdown was a calculated editorial decision. The prominent scheduling and promotion of *Car Share* was a response to a generalised moment of need. In the Corporation's own words, the show was 'brought back to BBC iPlayer to help keep people entertained during these unprecedented times' (BBC 2020).

The omnipresence of Zoom conversations during the pandemic created a new aesthetic of intimacy on media screens. As well as the extensive mediation of work and social life that many people experienced, audiences became used to seeing conventional TV programmes being filmed in the living rooms, kitchens and offices of presenters, panellists, celebrities and interviewees. Whether news bulletins or quiz shows, television was often stripped back and defined by small screen aesthetics out of necessity in 2020. In one sense *Car Share* stood apart from these constraints, a reminder of how television, and life more generally, used to look and behave. However, the intimacy of *Car Share* translated well to the moment. Expanding on TV's capacity to deliver a 'warm bath of nostalgia', Red Bee Media made the following observation as part of its report on audiences in lockdown:

> We've seen increased daily streaming of pre-loved series, old cartoons, comedy sketches and classic sports matches.

And that's not just because there's not new stuff available (there's loads). It's because right now we crave familiar characters, punchlines and final match scores that we can be sure of. (2020: 23)

*Car Share* fulfilled a craving for familiar characters and punchlines; it re-enlivened the routine of John and Kayleigh and offered humour in the upbeat striving of 'Brillington College – where brilliant is almost our name' (a poignant gag given that schools and colleges across the UK were closed). Together with the surety of a happy ending, the show offered the restorative pleasure of watching social proximity rather than distance. Nostalgia was always part of the show's comedic impetus, with the 1980s providing a music and cultural touchstone. In 2020, however, the sitcom would embody a more immediate and unforeseen nostalgia, evoking memories of the social life of cars before the cataclysm of Covid-19.

## Conclusion: quotidian comedy

Premiering the first series of *Car Share* on iPlayer was an experiment for the BBC. Adopting the Netflix strategy of making all episodes available at once, the sitcom signalled a step in the BBC's re-conception of iPlayer 'from catch-up TV to online TV' in the 2010s (Grainge and Johnson 2018). Increasingly, BBC iPlayer was developed as an 'entertainment destination' where people might start their viewing journey rather than just use it to catch up on shows missed. In a period when the boundaries between broadcast and digital television were becoming more fluid, iPlayer was positioned to become, in the words of the BBC's Director General Tony Hall, 'the best online TV service in the world, and the front door to many people to the whole BBC' (Hall 2013). As the first new BBC1 series to be released on iPlayer in its entirety, the ordinariness of *Car Share* was indicative. Rather than select a flagship natural history programme or a prestige serial drama for the iPlayer content trial, the BBC used an everyday sitcom about the social life of cars. In opening the door to box-sets, the BBC put stock in the populist humour of passengering.

As discussed in this chapter, 'ordinariness' and 'ordinary television' are not pejorative terms; within television studies they point to the treatment of the mundane in TV representation. This finds many expressions, from non-scripted reality television and lifestyle programmes focusing on homes and gardens through to clip shows using home video and surveillance footage. In Frances Bonner's account, ordinary television is not generally the kind of show that features on the cover of the *Radio Times*, as was the case with the final episode of *Car Share* (26 May 2018). Television Studies has tended to favour a limited number of genres – news, children's programming, drama of various sorts – and *Car Share* belongs in the list of the privileged; it is a fictional programme featuring a well-known star broadcast in primetime. And yet comedy remains a far less examined category of television than one might expect given its huge popularity. This final chapter has focused on a car-based comedy concerned with the ordinary in a TV genre (the sitcom) that still remains in the slow lane of academic television analysis.

In the introduction to their anthology *British TV Comedies*, Juergen Kamm and Birgit Neumann reflect: 'it is surprising that relatively little academic work has as yet been done on a genre that is as popular and entertaining as it is intellectually challenging. Up to now, British TV comedies, including their generic variety, filmic history, humour politics and cultural impact, have rarely been studied in a comprehensive and systematic manner' (2015: 1). Whether or not one agrees with Mark Lawson's suggestion that *Car Share* 'will stand as one of the highest achievements of twenty-first century TV comedy', it certainly became one of the most popular sitcoms in the UK in the 2010s. As well as maintaining high ratings, the show was voted third in an online poll conducted by the *Radio Times* of the 'top twenty' sitcoms of the twenty-first century.[14] One TV critic described Kay, affirmatively, as 'a crowd-pleaser rather than a boundary-pusher', a performer who is unashamedly populist in developing a comedy universe of 'mums, dads and nannas, package holidays and net curtains, wedding receptions and flicking the Vs' (Hogan 2017a: 34).

As an exploration of the ordinary, *Car Share* belongs in Kay's quotidian universe; it is a BAFTA-winning comedy about the mundanity of the commute. However, the programme is also a story of friendship and romance, a naturalistic sitcom about the affinities that people find through conversation, gossip, music, dreaming, remembering, singing and skiving in the shared space of a car. When *Car Share* was first released in 2015, the TV and food critic Grace Dent (2015) described herself laughing 'loudly and gracelessly' at Kay's 'pared-down comedy'. Watching the whole series immediately after it became available on iPlayer, Dent described her viewing in terms of gluttony, commenting: 'I gobbled up the whole series in one afternoon. One serving wasn't nearly enough'. She finished her review with the entreaty, 'more episodes please, BBC, I've finished all of these ones' (Ibid.). Dent's review taps into the language of 'binge-watching' that was mobilised around the show. As mentioned at the start of this chapter, the Controller of BBC Comedy affirmed that Kay hoped that people would 'warm to the core relationship of Kayleigh and John through binge-watching' (cited in Lawson 2018). By premiering the show on BBC iPlayer, audiences were able to view consecutive episodes of the series in a single sitting if they were so inclined. In discursive terms, this connects sitcom with the concept of 'binge-worthy' television.

'Binge-viewing' became a prevalent metaphor for TV viewing in the 2010s (Jenner 2018). Following Netflix, which deployed the term for marketing purposes even before the company became a streaming giant, the BBC assumed the language of 'binge-worthy' shows on iPlayer. In analytic terms, Graeme Turner argues that binge-viewing has become a 'handy proxy' for describing contemporary TV consumption, used by industry and academic researchers alike. However, he argues that the term is imprecise and freighted in describing how audiences watch television. Reflecting on academic use of the bingeing metaphor, he notes that 'the most curious aspect of television studies' examination of binge-viewing is how little research has involved observing actual audience behaviour and how much discussion of binge-viewing has been prosecuted through the analysis of a select group of television texts, most commonly *Breaking Bad* and *House of Cards*' (Turner 2019: 6). This chapter makes no claim to examine 'actual' viewing habits (or 'audience needs') as they relate to *Car Share*. However, Turner's point about the critical discussion of binge-viewing is telling. By using a 'select group of television texts', mainly high-end drama, he points to specific kinds of programme, genre and approach that take precedence in Television Studies.

The idea of *Car Share* as 'binge-worthy' departs from the critical propensity to equate 'addictive' shows, and compulsive viewing, with complex serial drama. While media scholars like Annette Hill (2019) and Beverley Skeggs and Helen Wood (2012) have explored the nature of audience engagement with reality television, among other live entertainment formats, it is less common in television studies to consider marathon viewing of shows about the mundane. This risks downplaying practices and relations of viewing with 'ordinary television', including shows that deal with ordinary relations with cars. I could reflect on watching consecutive episodes of a docusoap called *Bangers and Cash* (Yesterday, 2019–present), for example, a car restoration show that I happened upon with friends one Sunday.[15] Or, like Grace Dent, I might point to the gobbling up of other TV shows that are neither prestigious nor complex but that are compulsive on their own terms. Of course, Turner's point is to move beyond personal anecdotes and to ground claims of viewing behaviour in empirical audience study. The discourse of bingeing around *Car Share* is suggestive, however. As the first BBC1 series to be offered online ahead of broadcast transmission, the distribution of *Car Share* tapped into the language of binge and repeat viewing. As the blurb of the DVD box-set of Series 1 and 2 proclaimed, 'wonderful, natural performances and beautiful, witty writing, makes this a joyous comedy that you'll want to watch time and time again'.

Possible to consume in the space of a whole afternoon, *Car Share* helps connect sitcom with discussions of marathon viewing, just as the programme's concern with the commute establishes pleasure in returning for the ride.

In Series 2 of *Car Share*, the opening episode refers to 'Carpool Karaoke' directly. Speaking to John on a mobile phone while beginning her commute on foot, Kayleigh remarks that she was 'awake for ages, sat up watching YouTube . . . kittens dancing and Carpool Karaoke'. John replies matter-of-factly on his car speakerphone, 'there's nothing but shit on YouTube and you sit up all night watching it'. As in *The Trip to Spain*, 'Carpool Karaoke' is used as an intertext for car-based comedy. In this case, however, the celebrity 'drive-and-sing' is not regaled as 'the big thing' by fellow screen stars finishing an expensive dinner, but casually dismissed by two supermarket employees making their way to work. The classed distinction between celebrities playing at commuting, and two white-collar workers navigating rush-hour traffic by necessity, is marked. Rather than see parallels with their own experience – two people driving to work, inhabiting a car, talking and singing, sharing space in the act of passengering – John and Kayleigh frame 'Carpool Karaoke' as a frothy YouTube fix on a par with cat videos. The digital short provides a foil, in other words, for constructing the ordinary, Corden's jocular ride to CBS studios half the world away from the unglamorous repeat journey to and from a retail shift.

Joe Moran writes that 'the road is almost a separate country, one that remains underexplored not because it is remote and inaccessible but because it is so ubiquitous and familiar' (2009: 8). Despite the pretence of workaday driving in 'Carpool Karaoke', the celebrity world is remote in this TV-digital hybrid, just as the journeys and destinations in *The Trip* remain inaccessible for most. Through its situation and story of courting, Kay's first series for the BBC celebrates the ubiquitous and familiar, as the history of TV sitcom often has. Through attention to everyday rituals of the road, *Car Share* is driven by the accidental poetry of the commute.

# Conclusion: Mobility and Media

In March 2020, two weeks before the UK entered a period of national lockdown in response to the coronavirus pandemic, I visited a special exhibition at the V&A museum in London called 'Cars: Accelerating the Modern World'. Travelling by taxi, train and underground from my home in Nottingham, two hours away, it was the last significant journey I would take for many months. The pandemic caused a deceleration in mobility across the modern world, an acute example of the 'global humbling' that Zadie Smith described (2020). Humbling is not a word generally associated with the impact of the car in modern culture. Acknowledging the role of the automobile in shaping global society, the V&A exhibit considered how 'over its short 130-year history, the car has become one of the most loved, contested and influential innovations in the world' (V&A 2020). As part of its 'rear-view mirror' on automotive history, the exhibition explored the centrality of automobiles in revolutionising manufacturing, transforming how we move, and in changing our cities, environment and economies. The curators were also alert to the function of popular media as part of the story, however. Throughout the twentieth century, and continuing today, the history of the automobile has been inseparable from the ads, films, print media and TV that have imagined cars and their place in modern life.

As mass phenomena of the modern world, the history of television and cars run adjacent; in each case early developments in production, technology and consumer use in the first half of the twentieth century laid the foundation for mainstream take-up mid-century onwards, leading to global ubiquity by the century's end. Critics such as Margaret Morse have explicitly theorised the socio-historical connection between television and car-based realms of experience such as the freeway and the shopping mall. Exploring sites and principles of 'privatized mobility' developing after World War Two, Morse offers a critique of mass culture that relates transportation, broadcasting and retailing to what she calls, pessimistically, an 'ontology of everyday distraction' (1990). Exploring the entwined history of television and cars would require a different, and much longer, book. *TV and Cars* is deliberately modest in scope but hopefully productive in bringing two fields of enquiry together that have sometimes passed each other by: the respective study of mobility and media. Building on new critical approaches articulating these different fields, a growing number of academics have pointed to the gains of bringing 'mobility studies' and 'media studies' together (Keightley and Reading 2014; Hildebrand 2018; Miller 2018).

In a useful summary, James Miller (2018) suggests that 'mobility' and 'media' are two fields but one subject. Drawing together perspectives, he notes that while mobility has become a significant feature of media experience, media has been increasingly embedded into practices of movement and transit. While devices like tablets and smartphones have extended the bounds of media mobility as never before, the presence of media screens in planes, trains, automobiles and other forms of itinerant space has become routine. In 1935, the art historian Rudolph Arnheim wrote an essay called 'A Forecast of Television' that argued that television is a relative of the motorcar and airplane in providing 'a means of transport for the mind' (Arnheim 2006: 188). Various critics in Television and Media Studies have used Arnheim's metaphor of cultural transportation to explore physical, as well as symbolic, modes of media mobility. David Morley (2010), for instance, has integrated Transport Studies and Communication Studies by relating television to histories and routeways of the shipping container box. Meanwhile Stephen Groening (2014) explores 'aerial circuits of television' in his transmedia study of inflight entertainment. As in these two accounts, James Miller reminds us that the 'lived relationship' between mobility and media should be understood historically. Specifically, he uses the case of the portable radio and in-car media to make clear the long history of mobile electronic media, both of which have origins dating back to the 1920s and 1930s. His wider point, capturing discrete concerns in Media Studies and Cultural Sociology, is the interaction of two different historical processes: the 'mobilization of media technologies' and the 'mediatization of transportation technologies' (Ibid.: 385). This book has drawn on different literatures within and around the study of television to consider how automobility has been represented on small screens, notably in the 2010s. In this brief conclusion, I consider the relation of screens, cars and my case examples to broader contexts, and politics, attending to the acceleration of media and automobility in contemporary culture.

Cars have long been a subject of screen representation. One of the earliest examples is Cecil B. Hepworth's *How it Feels to Be Run Over* (1900), a single-shot film creating the illusion of a motorcar colliding with a spectator/camera. In a reversal of this perspective, many automobiles have been transformed into mobile cameras themselves in recent decades. With the proliferation of dashcams, collisions are now often seen from the perspective of the driver rather than the spectator, miniature cameras fitted to capture road incidents for policing and insurance purposes. While in-car videos have been used in police squad cars in the US since the mid-late 1990s, the RAC estimated that nine per cent of drivers in the UK (2.9 million motorists) had fitted dashcams to their vehicles in 2015, resulting in millions of mundane journeys being filmed (Barkham 2015). These auto-visuals have inspired factual entertainment genres, in-car video giving rise to programmes like *Police Camera Action!* (ITV, 1994–2010) among other examples of the emergency service docusoap. More recently, the mediation of motoring on smartphones has spawned a social media boom in serendipitous crash footage. This trend was playfully adapted in an Australian web series called *Content* (ABC, 2019) that began with a scene of a wannabe influencer simultaneously livestreaming and driving and flipping her car. Released on YouTube, Facebook, Instagram and iView, and filmed vertically in portrait ratio to be viewed more easily on smartphones, the clip of the self-defined #Flipgirl went viral when some viewers mistook the moment as a real accident (Meade 2019).

In terms of automotive design, screen media is now routinely built into car dashboards and control surfaces; automobile interiors have become a software interface where the driver is able to engage with a host of digital and touchscreen features to control the environment and performance of the vehicle. Merging audio with visual and text display, and with information, communication and entertainment frequently accessed through voice and wireless control, the car dashboard has become a digital cockpit. In some vehicles, display information can even appear in the windscreen, visual data commingling with the view of the road. Considering the future of driverless vehicles, beyond the design of the dashboard, James Miller observes, 'the application of artificial intelligence and advanced telematics is now producing the autonomous automobile, a still more media-saturated mobile environment that will create, to varying degrees and lengths of time, driverless automobility, perhaps the ultimate realisation of dwelling in the car' (Ibid.: 388). Developing this point, David Bissel et al. suggest that autonomous cars will reconfigure both driving *and* passengering as vehicles are fully realised as 'mobile entertainment and communication pods' (2020: 119). If, as they suggest, 'autonomous vehicles are one of the most highly anticipated technological developments of our time' (Ibid.: 117), promising greater flexibility for work and leisure activities, the predicted cultural impact of driverless cars is not simply around machine intelligence and smart transport systems, but the new social life of cars.

The exhibition at the V&A in 2020 was positioned at a 'turning point' in automotive design. As a curatorial provocation, the first narrative panel asserted that 'as new technologies evolve, consumer habits shift and oil supplies dwindle, the future of mobility is up for grabs'. The examples of television comedy in this book hint at this future, but only obliquely. This is especially the case in environmental terms, where the shift in people's relationship with cars is conferred in the activity of car sharing itself. The concept of ride sharing and carpooling became more prevalent in the 2010s as environmental debate became more urgent and the language of 'climate emergency' took hold. It is not incidental that 'Carpool Karaoke' and *Car Share* both used ride sharing as a conceit. In major urban centres like Los Angeles, London and Sydney, traffic density has led to congestion charging and ride sharing schemes becoming matters of municipal policy, including measures to limit the number of vehicles on roads.

Corden needs a passenger in 'Carpool Karaoke' so that he can use a 'high-occupancy vehicle lane' (HOV), a restricted traffic lane reserved for the exclusive use of vehicles with a driver and one or more passengers. Three-person carpools were introduced permanently in Los Angeles in 1976, with national expansion of HOV lanes in the 1990s following policy amendments to the Clean Air Act that actively promoted their construction and use. Ride sharing in 'Carpool Karaoke' is part of well-established commuting practice in Los Angeles in this regard. Carpooling is far less common in the UK. A government sponsored review of the 'UK passenger road transport network' in 2019 concluded that 'new shared modes of transport (such as ride sourcing and ride sharing) are making significant inroads only in particular geographical areas, primarily in London' (Angeloudis and Stettler 2019: 65).[1] Set in Greater Manchester, rather than London, John and Kayleigh participate in a car share scheme as an experiment by their supermarket employer rather than as the result of local transport policy. Asked by Kayleigh why their employer has introduced the scheme, John replies, 'apparently it's good for the environment . . . that and we haven't got enough car parking space at work'. Reducing the number of cars involved in workplace commuting is an environmental issue but also, of course, an easy win for big companies when it comes to 'greenwashing' corporate values (as well as freeing up parking bays).

Discussion about the environmental crisis became acute in the 2010s. However, the impact of petrol/diesel cars is rarely called into question in the auto-centric shows I consider, despite SUVs – a major source of $CO_2$ emissions and environmental bad faith – featuring prominently in *The Trip* and 'Carpool Karaoke'. While 'Carpool Karaoke' seemingly accepts that celebrities can and must travel in SUVs, *The Trip* series refers to the 'monster gas guzzler' that it features, but only fleetingly, and amidst shots of Range Rovers that have the gleaming look of car advertising throughout. In many ways, *The Trip* plays with contradictions of liberal discourse when it comes to SUVs and green politics. Mirroring the show's conceit as a commission by a left-leaning newspaper, a feature on *The Trip to Greece* that appeared in *The Guardian Magazine* helps illustrate these incongruities (Barton 2020). The magazine included a host of 'weekending' articles on the environment, wellbeing and sustainable ways of living and gardening, but also numerous full-page ads for SUVs. This included a 'paid content' magazine cover promoting Subaru's Forester 4x4 with the strapline, 'Don't be a dummy: why playing it safe is the new bold'. In television and print media, as in consumer culture more broadly, the future of mobility had not moved beyond the allure of the privatised fortress by 2020, even for those who might be most ready to identify as environmentally conscious.

Of course, the purpose of television comedy in each of my examples is to provide humour in the habitat of cars rather than to drive climate ecology critique. And yet, TV comedy can help reflect and disseminate cultural values. There is a latent sense of the environmental impact of cars in *The Trip*, 'Carpool Karaoke' and *Car Share*, but more through allusions to contemporary discourses of automobility (the virtues of hybrid engines, the value of car sharing) than via explicit comedy observations, satire or parody. As cultural and representational forms, the shows can be understood, more specifically, as portraits of automotive passengering. In different ways, they use the situation of the car to explore intimacies of human interaction and behaviour. The confined space of the automobile, conveyed through the small screen aesthetics of television, provides a way to comprehend the social dimension of mobility that comes with 'being together' in cars.

Predictably, masculinity is persistent in the gendering of cars in this context, extending the gendered space of TV comedy to a domain (motor vehicles) also frequently cast as male. This privileging of male experience is not inevitable or prescribed. Providing a vantage on female automobility, the broadcaster Victoria Coren Mitchell hosted a BBC radio series in the 2010s titled *Women Talking About Cars* (BBC Radio 4, 2016–present). The premise was to interview famous women in British media life – Olivia Coleman, Germaine Greer, Jennifer Saunders, among others – and invite them to look at their lives from the perspective of the cars they have known. Themes emerge in this series that differ from the representation of automobility in television's male-driven vehicles. During the interview with Germaine Greer, for instance, Coren Mitchell explained that her idea for the series was to find 'a way of loving cars that isn't really about its top speed or its carburettor but a means of escape, comfort and refuge' (TX 21 December 2016). The feelings that Coren Mitchell describes are certainly not limited to female auto experience. I can find echoes in my own history of car ownership. However, I sense that feelings of 'escape, comfort and refuge' were more acute for my younger sister, whose first car (an aubergine-coloured Ford Fiesta that she called 'auberghini') suddenly enabled her to get around our rough and tumble city, even when dark.

Focusing on the 2010s provides a way of examining different 'turning points' in discussion about the future of mobility and media. In automotive terms, conventions of driving and passengering were (and remain) firmly in place in the first decades of the twenty-first century. However, the prospect of 'autonomous automobility', symbolised by the launch of the self-driving Google Car in 2010, was becoming more credible (Elliot 2019: 135–41). In January 2021, NBC ordered a pilot of a new sitcom called *American Auto*, a show about a floundering group of executives trying to rediscover the identity of a Detroit-based car manufacturer in a rapidly changing industry. Although the future of driverless cars remains to be seen, it is feasible that in years and decades to come the auto industry will be shaped by new tech players, and that the driver will *become* a passenger in the habitat of autonomous vehicles. This will lead to profound transformations in how people spend time on the road and what automobility means. Whatever the likes of Google and Tesla have in store, and the reality of testing and regulation underlying the hype about a driverless tomorrow, the representation of passengering in the 2010s has a certain historical resonance. We are nearing the end of a particular relationship with the petrol-driven, pedal-controlled automobile, and television provides a means of capturing values, experiences and assumptions involved in current ways of 'feeling the car' (Sheller 2004).

The 2010s would also represent a 'turning point' for the future of the TV industry, which many see as a period when screen culture moved into a different digital gear (Cunningham and Craig 2019; Johnson 2019). The 'mobilisation of media technologies' in the 2010s had major consequences for the business models and distribution systems of the television industry, facilitating an environment where 'platform mobility' (Tryon 2013) shaped, and continues to affect, the way that media entertainment is produced, circulated, consumed and shared. Of the case examples in this book, 'Carpool Karaoke' is the most direct response to the TV-digital ecology that grew in the 2010s. As the expression of a new micro-genre (the 'drive-and-talk'), short-form TV developed an aesthetic of mobility in conceit but also in the way that it trafficked between television and YouTube.

*The Trip* and *Car Share* would experiment with cross-media (television and film) and cross-platform (broadcast and streaming) release, but they are more conventional TV programmes in genre, length and style. Notably, they speak to developments in contemporary television situation comedy. While *The Trip* blends gastronomic, automotive and improvisational genres in a playful meta-comedy about masculinity, middle-age and taste, *Car Share* belongs to a tradition of sitcom addressing the ordinary. The two programmes are different in their concerns but they both illustrate a *mobilisation* of the trend towards naturalism that Brett Mills (2009) has identified as a feature of contemporary sitcom. With developments in mobile digital cameras, automobiles have become a more frequent 'situation' for TV comedy, ranging from scenic drives along the Amalfi coast to mundane commutes on Manchester A-roads. Filming inside cars is by no means new, but the prevalence of passengering in contemporary comedy entertainment – from sitcoms and talk shows to web series and vlogging – has given the intersection of mobility and media a new vernacular, as well as vehicular, status.

It is possible to draw different lines of comparison between the three case examples in this book: as TV reframed beyond broadcast contexts, as shows defined by spatial confinement, as series based on the informality of talk, as productions made possible by mobile cameras, as performances of unabashed singing, and as vehicles steered literally by men. Each case is a vehicular 'two-hander', a show filmed in a car focusing on the interaction between driver and passenger. In finding humour in the habitat of cars, they provide different ways of thinking about automobility and the forms of talk and social interaction that take place inside vehicles. At the same time, each show explores TV's representation of automobility as 'uneventful' rather than action-packed or about the vehicle itself. By dwelling on cars, and our dwelling *in* cars, *The Trip*, 'Carpool Karaoke' and *Car Share* provide ways of considering small screen intimacy; they suggest how confinement in the mobile space of the car has lent itself to television's expression of the contemplative, proximate and commonplace.

I began this book by suggesting alternative ways of exploring the relationship between TV and cars. In analytic terms, I have chosen a particular route and perhaps not the most obvious one for readers expecting more on the way that cars feature in drama, sport or lifestyle shows. It is indicative that the index for this book includes entries for 'singing' and 'dogging' as readily as 'Clarkson' or 'Formula 1'. In venturing a theme, I have sought to mix the fuel of media studies and the air of mobility studies to create a combustion of sorts. It would be nice to end this book suggesting engines for discussion, but I am conscious of pushing the mechanics of this metaphor too far. Cars are a heuristic device for examining contemporary comedy entertainment and the sociology of passengering. It could be that the word 'heuristic' makes you want to ask, pleadingly at this point, 'are we nearly there yet'? As a child, my sister was known for this question at the start of any unfamiliar journey. I have taken 'B' roads rather than highways to explore the theme of TV and cars but I hope, in the spirit of a good spotter's guide, you have spied something interesting during the ride.

# Notes

## Introduction

1  *Starsky and Hutch* was first shown on BBC1 in 1976, scheduled on Saturday evenings at 9pm. By the time I was old enough to watch the show in the early 1980s, it had moved to slots on Friday (9.25pm) and Monday (7.40pm).
2  The BBC took the decision not to renew Clarkson's contract after he physically assaulted a *Top Gear* producer over the provision of hot food at the end of a day's filming. This incident was consistent with the brand of 'belligerent masculinity' that Clarkson helped build into the tonal address of *Top Gear*. As Philip Drake and Angela Smith note, *Top Gear* was characterised by 'discursive slipperiness' in the show's contrarian banter and protest masculinity, the programme's political views around such topics as climate change and congestion charging cast as 'part of the humour' (Drake and Smith 2016).
3  Thanks to my cousin, and original car enthusiast, John Bartlett for rescuing this memory.
4  In 2011, the vehicles were sold to an American collector and the museum relocated to the Miami Auto Museum, where it formed a permanent 'Cars of the Stars' exhibit. My thanks to Andrew Shepherd for drawing my attention to this collection.
5  Road trips provide a popular conceit for television series and specials. Among British comedians alone, this has included Stephen Fry driving across America in a London taxi (*Stephen Fry in America*, BBC1, 2008), Jennifer Saunders sharing memories with the actor Michael Sheen in an E-Type Jaguar (*Jennifer Saunders' Memory Lane*, ITV, 2020) and a fictional Christmas road trip, starring Stephen Merchant, where a father drives the length of the country with an annoying neighbour to buy a prized toy unicorn for his daughter (*Click and Collect*, BBC1, 2019).
6  I am concerned in this book with 'Carpool Karaoke' as a segment of *The*

*Late Late Show with James Corden* (CBS, 2015–present) rather than as a standalone show for Apple TV, *Carpool Karaoke: The Series* (Apple Music/ TV, 2017–present). As such, I designate the segment using inverted commas to distinguish it from the online TV show, although I use italics in the heading of Chapter 2 for title consistency and to indicate the status of 'Carpool Karaoke' as content of its own.

7   To avoid a clutter of broadcaster/dates for these shows, details are provided in individual chapters when the shows are discussed.

8   Assessing the impact of new technology on the delivery of media content, Brett Mills refers to experiments with 'satcom' in the late 2000s (2009: 140). Describing situation comedy delivered by satellite navigation systems in cars, he gives the example of *230 Miles of Love* (2008), 'moving audio content' which constructed a comic narrative through site-specific sketches linked to the M6 motorway in the UK. While satcom did not take off in the decade to come, mobile comedies – shows set in cars that could be consumed as digital shorts or podcasts through smartphones – did gain traction, as discussed in Chapter 2.

9   My thanks to Mark Gallagher for introducing me to this highly improbable sitcom.

## Chapter 1

1   Cardwell notes that the 4:3 aspect ratio associated with the traditional proportions of the television image remained the norm in Europe until the late 1990s, whereupon a new widescreen 16:9 ratio began to dominate. This was encouraged by television set producers selling ever bigger screens with the digital switchover to HDTV.

2   In this chapter, I follow Michael Allen and Janet McCabe's (2012) analysis of *The Trip* by differentiating the media selves of Coogan and Brydon from the heightened fictionalised versions of these constructs as 'Coogan' and 'Brydon' in the series.

3   As a niche independent film, *The Trip* was distributed by the American production and distribution company IFC. It took $1.84 million in theatrical box office revenue and was also released through video-on-demand (Saperstein 2011).

4   The decision to release *The Trip* and its sequels as a festival film may seem to contradict Winterbottom's claim about the need for 'plot' in film comedy. In this case, however, having 'no story' gave the film versions identity as quirky, independent features. In reviewing the movie version of *The Trip to Spain* for *The Atlantic*, David Sims wrote, 'the instalments barely count as films at all – they're cut-down versions of a sporadic, six-episodes-

per-season television series that airs in the UK. But the director Michael Winterbottom, a movie veteran who enjoys blurring the lines between fiction and reality, makes each entry feel like a complete, satisfying narrative' (Sims 2017).

5 *The Trip* points to changes in the production and commissioning environment of the contemporary British TV comedy industry. Ever since the 1990 Broadcasting Act introduced a 25 per cent independent production quota for all UK terrestrial channels, the BBC has looked to the independent sector for much of its comedy commissioning. In 2007, a regulatory provision called the 'Window of Creative Competition' further enabled independent companies to go head-to-head with in-house BBC producers for another 25 per cent of television commissions (Mills and Horton 2016: 34).

6 Responding to the revival of scripted comedy in British television, Sky appointed the BBC's Controller of Comedy Commissioning, Lucy Lumsden, to become its first Head of Comedy in 2009. Her move, and the defection of *The Trip to Spain*, would indicate the satellite provider's increasing investment in comedy during the 2010s. Sky launched a dedicated comedy channel in 2020 (Sky Comedy), although this was comprised mostly of imported programming from US networks and premium channels such as NBC, HBO and Showtime.

7 In the last episode of *The Trip to Greece*, 'Coogan' disconcerts 'Brydon' by taking the Range Rover off-road, accelerating across a deserted beach leaving behind plumes of sand. The act and image that leads 'Coogan' to observe, 'this is like *Top Gear* without the prehistoric Neanderthal views'.

8 Winterbottom used the road as a motif in the political docudrama *The Road to Gauntanamo* (2006) as well as *On the Road* (2016), a docufiction following the life of British indie band Wolf Alice on their tour bus.

9 Experimenting with 'branded content', Volvo used a mix of traditional and transmedia promotion to tell the story of a primary school teacher driving inner-city children to surf in the ocean for the first time. Without irony, the 'defiant pioneer' was in this case a teacher using an SUV to enable lessons in the natural world.

10 The commercial features a driver 'questing' at the wheel of vintage Honda vehicles that become more sleek and technically advanced in each successive shot: a scooter followed by a dune buggy, convertible, roadster, racing car, sports bike, powerboat and a hot air balloon. The ad was filmed against scenic backdrops in New Zealand and Iguaza Falls in South America.

11 Across the series, Larry's persona is linked to vehicles ranging from golf carts to a Toyota Prius with stories ranging from his investment in a ludicrous car periscope to getting stuck, slapstick-fashion, in a car wash.

12  Coogan took part on *Top Gear* three times before publicly chastising Jeremy Clarkson and his co-presenters in 2011 for recycling racist clichés about Mexicans in one episode, something he said was reprehensible given that *Top Gear* is frequently seen overseas as 'the public face of the BBC' (Coogan 2011).

13  As a parent, I have had some of the most rewarding conversations with my children during car journeys, and have learnt much about my boys' thoughts, friendships, feelings, interests, hopes and jokes in the process of giving lifts. I have even chosen to have certain conversations with my children in the car, precisely because the dynamic of talking and interacting in the front and back seats (including the ability to look ahead or out of the window) made them easier, less formal, more open. Of course, this has not stopped either of my boys wearing headphones and playing with their mobile phones for extended lengths of time while I act as a barely acknowledged chauffeur!

14  In an early episode of *Modern Family* (Season 2, Episode 1) the Dunphy family park their car at a woodland viewpoint over Los Angeles. A slapstick sequence ensues where calm is replaced by in-car pandemonium as Luke threatens to puke fast food, Hayley sees a spider in the back and accidentally pulls the front seatbelt across her Dad's neck, the windows won't open, the air-con sends billows of dust into Phil and Claire's face, and everyone jumps out, leaving the car to roll gently but unstoppably over a steep bank.

15  Roel Puijk (2015) examines how 'slow television' developed from attempts by the Norwegian Public Broadcasting Company to develop new programme formats and cross-media concepts. *Hurtigruten* not only attracted unexpectedly large television audiences, the programme also saw high levels of audience interactivity and social media engagement through Twitter and Facebook.

16  My thanks to Darren and Ellen Tobin for introducing me to the slow pleasures of this series.

17  In the audiobook stemming from their fishing series, Mortimer and Whitehouse discuss how they pitched the programme to the BBC's factual rather than comedy department, the BBC commissioner purportedly observing 'it's like *The Trip* but you guys are real'.

## Chapter 2

1  In February 2018, Seinfeld won a copyright infringement dispute against a former colleague who claimed he had originally conceived the idea for *Comedians in Cars Getting Coffee* in 2002, pitched as 'Two Stupid Guys in

a Stupid Car Driving to a Stupid Town'. Llewellyn explained that the idea for *Carpool* originated with a drive that he filmed with the comedian David Baddiel in 1998.
2  The first season of *Comedians in Cars Getting Coffee* was criticised for its lack of non-white, non-male guests, and 'for a perceived inability to relate to viewers who are not as prosperous as its creator' (Itzkoff 2015). As seasons progressed, a more diverse roster of guests featured in terms of age, ethnicity, sexual orientation and gender, from Aziz Anzari and Trevor Noah to Ellen DeGeneres and Margaret Cho.
3  Before Corden, *The Late Late Show* was presented by Craig Ferguson between 2005–14. Part of the reason for embracing digital was the success of the show's competitor *The Tonight Show with Jimmy Fallon*, which had used web video and YouTube as a 'growth engine' of late-night talk since 2009 (McNutt 2017: 578).
4  At the time of writing, Adele's appearance remains the most watched of all 'Carpool Karaoke' videos, garnering 225 million views in four years. The other most popular videos over the same period include One Direction (169 million), Justin Bieber (154 million), Sia (135 million), Selena Gomez (108 million) and Bruno Mars (127 million). The majority of 'Carpool Karaoke' videos currently range between views of 23 million (Madonna) and 79 million (Michelle Obama).
5  As part of this 2016 deal, *The Late Late Show* was promoted on McDonald's cups and wrappers for six weeks across the US, 'Carpool Karaoke' creating drive-thru marketing opportunities for the broadcast show.
6  Corden's star persona differed in the UK. When returning home in the late 2010s to present the sports-based panel show *A League of Their Own* (Sky1, 2010–present), the team captains, Jamie Redknapp and Freddy Flintoff, would delight in teasing Corden for being a 'Hollywood wanker'. Corden's meteoric fame in the US elicited a mix of admiration and envy in the UK, parodied by 'Brydon' and 'Coogan' in *The Trip to Spain* as discussed in Chapter 1.
7  Cars have become a setting for numerous influencer videos in the new screen ecology. The output of a YouTube star like MrBeast, for instance, often features automobiles as the centrepiece of expensive stunts, such as giving away forty cars to his forty millionth subscriber. However, vlogs also take place inside vehicles, with vlog channels like *Dad V Girls* using the family car to talk to followers and set challenges such as the drive-thru based 'letting the person in front of us decide what we eat'.
8  In different episodes of Robert Llewellyn's *Carpool*, TV industry passengers occasionally discuss the business of filming in cars, Craig Charles explaining that the soap opera *Coronation Street* (ITV, 1960–present) normally

uses a 'low-loader' when filming car scenes, and David Baddiel explaining the special permissions required when filming on a public highway with a camera on the bonnet.
9 Although *The Big Bang Theory* is a studio-based sitcom, it frequently includes scenes in cars, filmed against a moving backscreen to help situate stories and character relations among its 'family of friends'.
10 Based on the idea of premium mini-shows (five to ten minutes in length) that could be viewed during the commute, Quibi launched in March 2020 but quickly folded despite investment of $1.75 billion and the involvement of talent such as Steven Spielberg, Idris Elba, Will Smith and Jennifer Lopez.

## Chapter 3

1 *Car Share* was created by Paul Coleman and Tim Reid and written by Reid, Peter Kay and Sian Gibson. The series was developed by Kay's production company Goodnight Vienna.
2 Tim Edensor (2004) reminds us that 'national motorscapes' are constituted differently, from the distinctive character of roadside fixtures (street lighting, telegraph poles, post-boxes, billboards) through to roadside flora and fauna. Edensor also notes that driving practices are often nationally particular, such as the accepted norm of horn-honking and criss-crossing on Indian roads compared with the more regulated order of Western highways. The 'anthropology of the road' is by no means uniform, in this sense, and relates in this chapter to the British national context.
3 These ads provide a paean to the ordinary, either drawing on familiar scenes in British life (having a curry, wedding discos, doorstep chat) or placing the 'ordinary man' of John Smith in elite competitions such as the Crufts dog show or platform diving. In the latter, two physically toned competitors in tight trunks execute complex twists and rotations before the portly figure of 'John Smith', sporting beach shorts, appears on the platform and scores top marks for his 'no nonsense' running bomb, replete with gigantic splash.
4 In best-selling DVDs of Kay's various stand-up shows, camera shots frequently cut away to members of the audience nudging and pointing to each other in fits of recognition. These include performances in venues ranging from Blackpool Tower to London's O2 Arena.
5 Kay has returned to cars and roads in different guises through his career. He played an inept getaway driver in a short called 'Two Minutes' for the comedy series *New Voices* (Granada, 1997) and voiced an absent-minded car mechanic in the children's TV series *Roary the Racing Car* (Five, CBBC, 2007–10). Kay also co-wrote and starred in the sitcom *Max and Paddy's*

*Road to Nowhere*, a caper following two bouncers from Bolton on the run in a campervan, a spin-off from *Phoenix Nights*.
6   My thanks to the cultural studies scholar and former inhabitant of Westhoughton, David Wright, for this observation.
7   In a self-referential scene, John tells a corny joke driving past a zebra in a safari park, the same gag that Peter Kay previously used to open one of his live arena shows ('what's black and white and eats like a horse?'). While *Car Share* is not a meta-comedy in the same way as *The Trip*, it plays liberally with popular cultural references and alludes to traditions of sitcom and light entertainment in the programme's more theatrical set-pieces.
8   The 'unscripted' episode of *Car Share* caused controversy on Twitter by reacting in a disbelieving way to a phone-in story by a transgender woman on Forever FM. This satirical moment underlined the more general heteronormativity of the series in the attitudes of the main characters.
9   Audience investment in the relationship between John and Kayleigh was such that fans of the show circulated an online petition after the inconclusive end of the second series (the previously described 'Kayleigh' music video scene) demanding a romantic resolution. The petition received 100,000 signatures.
10  In a parallel effort to give people cheer, Kay made a new version of his iconic 'Amarillo' video (first made for Comic Relief in 2005), this time accompanied by nurses and doctors fighting the pandemic rather than light entertainment celebrities.
11  The BBC's 'Culture in Quarantine' campaign was launched at the start of the UK national lockdown as a series of commissions in arts and culture that ran across platforms. Designed to support the UK creative sector in a time of crisis, and provide cultural experiences through television, iPlayer and radio, it included curated programming around theatre, live music, galleries, collections, art and literature.
12  Kelly tracked 21 genre categories tagged by the BBC on iPlayer. This also included 'news' (169 records), 'sport' (539), 'lifestyle' (934) and 'food' (444).
13  My thanks to J. P. Kelly for scraping the data on *Car Share* using the methodology outlined in his article, '"Recommended for You": A Distant Reading of BBC iPlayer' (2021).
14  The poll (of 14,000 people) was based on a shortlist selected by *Radio Times* critics and experts from the British Film Institute (BBC 2016). *Car Share* was voted third behind *Mrs Brown's Boys* (BBC1, 2011–present) and *The Office*.
15  Coincidentally, *Bangers and Cash*, about a family-run car auctioneer in North Yorkshire, is narrated by Toby Foster, a British stand-up comedian

who appeared in *Phoenix Nights* as well as *That Peter Kay Thing* and *Max and Paddy's Road to Nowhere*.

## Conclusion

1 'Ride sharing' and 'car sharing' are distinguished in the terminology of this government transport review. Ride sharing is taken to refer to journeys where two or more people share a car and travel together towards a common destination, the key objective being to share a vehicle and the cost of a trip. Car sharing, on the other hand, refers to car clubs where users have access to vehicles for an annual membership fee. On these terms, *Peter Kay's Car Share* is, strictly speaking, about ride sharing.

# Bibliography

Allen, Michael and Janet McCabe (2012), 'Imitations of lives: ageing men, vocal mimicry and performing celebrity in *The Trip*', *Celebrity Studies* 3.2: 150–63.
Allison, Deborah (2012), *The Cinema of Michael Winterbottom*, Lanham: Lexington Books.
Angeloudis, Panagiotis and Marc Stettler (2019), *Review of the UK Passenger Road Transport Network*, London: Government Office for Science.
Arnheim, Rudolph (2006), *Film as Art*, Berkeley: University of California Press.
Barkham, Patrick (2015), 'The road to Britain's dashcam boom', *The Guardian*, 12 October, <https://www.theguardian.com/technology/shortcuts/2015/oct/12/dashcams-dashboard-cameras-dramatic-crashes-safer-roads> (last accessed 9 March 2021).
Barton, Laura (2014), 'It's just the two of them – again', *The Observer Food Monthly*, 19 January, p. 20.
Barton, Laura (2020), 'Twenty-four hour Plato people', *The Guardian Magazine*, 15 February, pp. 14–20.
BBC (2016), 'Mrs Brown's Boys named best British sitcom in audience poll', bbc.co.uk, 23 April, <https://www.bbc.co.uk/news/newsbeat-37162569> (last accessed 20 December 2020).
BBC (2020) 'Lots of box sets coming to BBC iPlayer to help keep people entertained', bbc.co.uk, 20 December <https://www.bbc.co.uk/mediacentre/latestnews/2020/bbc-iplayerboxsets> (last accessed 20 December 2020).
Bennett, James and Niki Strange (eds) (2011), *Television as Digital Media*, Durham: Duke University Press.
Berg, Maggie and Barbara K. Seeber (2016), *The Slow Professor*, Toronto: University of Toronto Press.
Bignell, Jonathan (2016), 'Cars, places and spaces in police drama', in Ruth McElroy (ed.), *Contemporary British Drama: Cops on the Box*, London: Routledge, pp. 123–36.

Bijsterveld, Karen, Eefje Cleophas and Stefan Krebs (2013), *Sound and Safe: A History of Listening Behind the Wheel*, Oxford: Oxford University Press.

Bissell, David, Thomas Birtchnell, Anthony Elliott and Eric L. Hsu (2020), 'Autonomous automobilities: the social impacts of driverless vehicles,' *Current Sociology* 68.1: 116–34.

Bonner, Frances (2003), *Ordinary Television*, London: Sage.

Bonner, Frances (2010), '*Top Gear*: why does the world's most popular programme not deserve scrutiny', *Critical Studies in Television* 5.1: 32–45.

Brownrigg, Mark and Peter Meech (2011), '"Music is half the picture": the soundworld of UK television idents', in Paul Grainge (ed.), *Ephemeral Media: Transitory Screen Culture from Television to YouTube*, London: British Film Institute, pp. 70–86.

Bryant, Andy and Charlie Mawer (2016), *The TV Brand Builders*, London: KoganPage.

Bull, Michael (2004), 'Automobility and the power of sound', *Theory, Culture & Society* 21.4/5: 243–59.

Cardwell, Sarah (2015), 'A sense of proportion: aspect ratio and the framing of television space', *Critical Studies in Television* 10.3: 8–100.

Chalaby, Jean K. (2016), *The Format Age*, Cambridge: Polity Press.

Coogan, Steve (2011), 'I'm a huge fan of Top Gear. But this time I've had enough', *The Observer*, 11 February, <https://www.theguardian.com/tv-and-radio/2011/feb/05/top-gear-offensive-steve-coogan> (last accessed 7 February 2021).

Conlan, Tara (2015), 'BBC's *Car Share* is highest-rated sitcom to premiere on any channel', *The Guardian*, 22 May, <https://www.theguardian.com/media/2015/may/22/car-share-becomes-highest-rated-sitcom-to-premiere-on-any-channel> (last accessed 18 January 2021).

Craig, David (2020), '*Peter Kay's Car Share* is returning for an audio only episode', *Radio Times*, 8 April, <https://www.radiotimes.com/news/tv/2020-04-08/peter-kays-car-share-comebac-audio-episode/> (last accessed 18 January 2021).

Creeber, Glen (2013), *Small Screen Aesthetics*, London: British Film Institute.

Cunningham, Stuart and David Craig (2019), *Social Media Entertainment*, New York: New York University Press.

Curtin, Michael, Jennifer Holt and Kevin Sanson (eds) (2014), *Distribution Revolution*, Berkeley: University of California Press.

*Daily Variety* (2010), 'The Trip', 17 September, np.

Dent, Grace (2015), '*Peter Kay's Car Share* made me genuinely LOL', *The Independent*, 3 May, <https://www.independent.co.uk/arts-entertainment/tv/reviews/grace-dent-tv-bbc-one-s-car-share-actually-made-me-laugh-out-loud-10215826.html> (last accessed 18 January 2021).

Dolan, Mark (2019), *Peter Kay Comedy Genius*, Channel 5, TX 20 December.
Donaldson, Lucy Fife and James Walters (2018), 'Inter(acting): television, performance and synthesis', *Critical Studies in Television* 13.3: 352–69.
Drake, Philip and Angela Smith (2016), 'Belligerent broadcasting, male antiauthoritarianism and anti-environmentalism: the case of *Top Gear* (BBC, 2002–2015)', *Environmental Communication* 10.6: 689–703.
Edensor, Tim (2004), 'Automobility and national identity: representation, geography and driving practice', *Theory, Culture & Society* 21.4/5: 101–20.
Elliott, Anthony (2019), *The Culture of AI*, London: Routledge.
Ellis-Petersen, Hannah (2017), 'Steve Coogan: *The Trip* is Last of the Summer Wine for Guardian readers', *The Guardian*, 1 March, <https://www.theguardian.com/tv-and-radio/2017/mar/01/steve-coogan-rob-brydon-the-trip-to-spain-is-last-of-the-summer-wine-for-guardian-readers> (last accessed 21 July 2020).
Evans, Elizabeth (2018), 'Transmedia distribution', in Matthew Freeman and Renira Rampazzo Gamabarato (eds), *Routledge Companion to Transmedia Studies*, London: Routledge, pp. 243–50.
Fane Saunders, Tristram (2016), 'Peter Kay's Bafta-winning *Car Share* confirmed for second series', *The Telegraph*, 1 June, <https://www.telegraph.co.uk/tv/2016/06/01/peter-kays-bafta-winning-car-share-confirmed-for-second-series/> (last accessed 18 January 2021).
Featherstone, Mike (2004), 'Automobilities: an introduction', *Theory, Culture & Society* 21.4/5: 1–24.
Gillibrand, Abigail (2020), 'Peter Kay "thrilled" as *Car Share* returns to BBC One: "It couldn't be shown at a better time"', *Metro*, 29 April, <https://metro.co.uk/2020/04/29/peter-kay-thrilled-car-share-returns-bbc-one-coronavirus-lockdown-12629066/?ito=cbshare> (last accessed 18 January 2021).
Grainge, Paul (ed.) (2011), *Ephemeral Media: Transitory Screen Culture from Television to YouTube*, London: British Film Institute.
Grainge, Paul (2017), '"Moments and opportunities": interstitials and the promotional imagination of BBC iPlayer', *Critical Studies in Television* 12.2: 139–55.
Grainge, Paul and Catherine Johnson (2015), *Promotional Screen Industries*, London: Routledge.
Grainge, Paul and Catherine Johnson (2018), 'From catch-up TV to online TV: digital broadcasting and the case of BBC iPlayer', *Screen* 59.1: 21–40.
Gray, Jonathan (2010), *Show Sold Separately: Promos, Spoilers and Other Media Paratexts*, New York: New York University Press.
Groening, Stephen (2014), *Cinema Beyond Territory: Inflight Entertainment and Atmospheres of Globalisation*, London: British Film Institute.

Hall, Tony (2013), 'Where next?', bbc.co.uk, 8 October, <http://www.bbc.co.uk/mediacentre/speeches/2013/tony-hall-vision.html> (last accessed 14 April 2014).

Haynes, Richard and Timothy Robeers (2020), 'The need for speed? A historical analysis of the BBC's post-war broadcasting of motorsport', *Historical Journal of Film, Radio and Television*, 40.2: 407–23.

Heritage, Stuart (2018), 'Driving profits: how the car-cam became comedy's favourite vehicle', *The Guardian*, 5 July, < https://www.theguardian.com/tv-and-radio/2018/jul/05/driving-profits-how-the-car-cam-became-comedys-favourite-vehicle> (last accessed 24 February 2021).

Heritage, Stuart (2019), '*Comedians in Cars Getting Coffee*: how Netflix totalled Seinfeld's star vehicle', *The Guardian*, 19 July, <https://www.theguardian.com/tv-and-radio/2019/jul/19/comedians-in-cars-getting-coffee-netflix-jerry-seinfeld-star-vehicle> (last accessed 30 October 2020).

Hildebrand, Julia M. (2018), 'Modal media: connecting media ecology and mobilities research', *Media, Culture & Society* 40.3: 348–64.

Hill, Annette (2019), *Media Experiences*, London: Routledge.

Hogan, Michael (2017a), 'Comedy grafter gets back in the driving seat', *The Observer*, 9 April, p. 34.

Hogan, Michael (2017b), '*The Trip to Spain*: middle-age, mortality and Mick Jagger', *The Telegraph*, 6 April, <https://www.telegraph.co.uk/tv/2017/04/06/trip-spain-middle-age-mortality-mick-jagger-review/> (last accessed 21 July 2020).

Holdsworth, Amy (2011), *Television, Memory and Nostalgia*, Basingstoke: Palgrave Macmillan.

Holt, Jennifer and Kevin Sanson (2014), *Connected Viewing*, New York: Routledge.

Husband, Stuart (2019), 'Alan Partridge: his rise and fall (and rise again), as told by his creators', *The Telegraph*, 25 February, <https://www.telegraph.co.uk/tv/0/alan-partridge-rise-fall-rise-told-creators/> (last accessed 21 July 2020).

Itzkoff, Dave (2015), 'Jerry Seinfeld, online force', *The New York Times*, 31 May, <https://www.nytimes.com/2015/05/31/arts/television/jerry-seinfeld-online-force.html> (last accessed 30 October 2020).

Jefferies, Mark (2015) 'Peter Kay creates whole new radio station for background noise in his new series', *The Mirror*, 21 April, <http://www.mirror.co.uk/tv/tv-news/peter-kay-creates-whole-new-5556783> (last accessed 20 August 2020)

Jenkins, Henry, Sam Ford and Joshua Green (2013), *Spreadable Media*, New York: New York University Press.

Jenner, Mareike (2018), *Netflix and the Re-invention of Television*. Basingstoke: Palgrave Macmillan.

Johnson, Catherine (2019), *Online TV*, London: Routledge.

Johnson, Catherine (2020a), 'TV viewing has surged during lockdown, but has become too technical for some new research', *The Conversation*, 4 May, <https://theconversation.com/tv-viewing-has-surged-during-lockdown-but-has-become-too-technical-for-some-new-research-136441> (last accessed 18 January 2021).

Johnson, Catherine (2020b), 'The appisation of television: TV apps, discoverability and the software, device and platform ecologies of the internet era', *Critical Studies in Television* 15.2: 165–82.

Johnson, Derek (ed.) (2018), 'Television guides and recommendations in a changing channel landscape', in Derek Johnson (ed.), *From Networks to Netflix*, New York: Routledge, pp. 3–22.

Jolly, Jasper (2020), 'Sales sink to lowest levels for 74 years', *The Guardian*, 6 May, p. 2.

Jones, Emma (2014), 'Living la Dolce Vita', *Independent*, 22 January, p. 36.

Jones, Jeffrey P. (2009), 'I want my talk TV: network talk shows in a digital universe', in Amanda D. Lotz (ed.), *Beyond Prime Time: Television Programming in the Post-Network Era*, New York: Routledge, pp. 14–35.

Kalyan, Rohan (2020), '"Don't you see what's going on here?" *Seinfeld* and Badiou on situations and events', *Television and New Media* 21.5: 493–509.

Kamm, Juergen and Birgit Neumann (2015), 'Introduction: the aesthetics and politics of British TV comedy', in Kamm and Neumann (eds), *British TV Comedies*, Basingstoke: Palgrave Macmillan, pp. 1–20.

Katz, Jack (1999), *How Emotions Work*, Chicago: University of Chicago Press.

Keightley, Emily and Anna Reading (2014), 'Mediated mobilities', *Media, Culture & Society* 36.3: 285–301.

Kelly, J. P. (2021), '"Recommended for you": A distant reading of BBC iPlayer', *Critical Studies in Television*, published online, forthcoming.

Kim, Jin (2012), 'The institutionalization of YouTube: from user-generated content to professionally-generated content', *Media, Culture & Society* 34.1: 53–67.

Klinger, Barbara (2006), *Beyond the Multiplex: Cinema, New Technologies, and the Home*, Berkeley: University of California Press.

Kommenda, Niko (2019), 'SUVs second biggest cause of emissions rise, figures reveal', *The Guardian*, 25 October, <https://www.theguardian.com/environment/ng-interactive/2019/oct/25/suvs-second-biggest-cause-of-emissions-rise-figures-reveal> (last accessed 21 July 2020).

Krewani, Angela (2015), 'Family life in front of the telly: *The Royle Family*', in Juergen Kamm and Birgit Neumann (eds), *British TV Comedies*, Basingstoke: Palgrave Macmillan, pp. 254–64.

Laurier, Eric and Hayden Lorimer (2012), 'Other ways: landscapes of commuting', *Landscape Research* 37.2: 207–24.

Laurier, Eric, Hayden Lorimer, Barry Brown et al (2008), 'Driving and "passengering": notes on the ordinary organization of car travel', *Mobilities* 3.1: 1–23.

Lawson, Mark (2018), 'Peter Kay's *Car Share* reaches end of the road', *The Guardian*, 28 May, <https://www.theguardian.com/culture/2018/may/28/peter-kays-car-share-reaches-end-of-the-road> (last accessed 18 January 2021).

Llewellyn, Robert (2010a), 'Carpool: David Baddiel', 5 February, <https://www.youtube.com/watch?v=_zf_3pKQVQA > (last accessed 30 October 2020).

Llewellyn, Robert (2010b), 'Carpool announcement', 30 June, <https://www.youtube.com/watch?v=dxChmIv4VZ4 > (last accessed 30 October 2020).

Llewellyn, Robert (2010c), 'Carpool on Dave launch', 31 October, <https://www.youtube.com/watch?v=of7AYSX1hYE> (last accessed 30 October 2020).

Lobato, Ramon (2019), *Netflix Nations*, New York: New York University Press.

Lobato, Ramon and Julian Thomas (2015), *The Informal Media Economy*, Cambridge: Polity Press.

Lochlann Jain, Sarah (2002), 'Urban errands: the means of mobility', *Journal of Consumer Culture* 2.3: 385–404.

Marx, Nick (2018), 'Comedy Central: transgressive femininities and reaffirmed masculinities', in Derek Johnson (ed.), *From Networks to Netflix*, New York: Routledge, pp. 177–98.

Marx, Nick (2019), *Sketch Comedy: Identity, Reflexivity, and American Television*, Bloomington: Indiana University Press.

Mason, Jennifer (2018), *Affinities: Potent Connections in Personal Life*, Cambridge: Polity Press.

McDonald, Paul (2009), 'Digital discords in the online media economy: advertising versus content versus copyright', in Pelle Snickars and Patrick Vonderau (eds), *The YouTube Reader*, Stockholm: National Library of Sweden, pp. 387–405.

McGlynn, Katya (2012), 'Jerry Seinfeld opens up about *Comedians In Cars Getting Coffee*: "This Is Just What We Like To Do"', *Huffington Post*, 23 August, <https://www.huffingtonpost.co.uk/entry/jerry-seinfeld-comedians-in-cars-getting-coffee> (last accessed 30 October 2020).

McGlynn, Katya (2014), 'Seinfeld schools Letterman on "Comedians in Cars," A.K.A. "the anti-show about a nonevent"', *Huffington Post*, 12 June, <https://www.huffingtonpost.co.uk/entry/jerry-seinfeld-david-letterman-comedians-in-cars-paley_n_5480298?ri18n=true> (last accessed 30 October 2020).

McNutt, Myles (2017), 'Classroom Instruments and Carpool Karaoke: ritual and collaboration in late night's YouTube era', *Television and New Media* 18.7): 569–88.

Meade, Victoria (2019), '#FlipGirl car crash video goes viral after clip from ABC show mistaken for real thing', *The Guardian*, 5 September, <https://www.theguardian.com/media/2019/sep/05/abc-clip-goes-viral-after-fictional-car-crash-mistaken-for-real-thing> (last accessed 9 March 2021).

Medhurst, Andy (2007), *A National Joke: Popular Comedy and English Cultural Identities*, London: Routledge.

Miller, James (2018), 'Media and mobility: two fields, one subject', *The Journal of Transport History* 39.3: 381–97.

Miller, Toby (2017), *Greenwashing Culture*, London: Routledge.

Mills, Brett (2004), 'Comedy verité: contemporary sitcom form', *Screen* 45.1): 63–78.

Mills, Brett (2009), *The Sitcom*, Edinburgh: Edinburgh University Press.

Mills, Brett (2015), 'Old jokes: *One Foot in the Grave*, comedy and the elderly', in Juergen Kamm and Birgit Neumann (eds), *British TV Comedies*, Basingstoke: Palgrave Macmillan, pp. 265–77.

Mills, Brett and Erica Horton (2016), *Creativity in the British Television Comedy Industry*, London: Routledge.

Mills, Brett and Mark Rimmer (2017), 'Pure and Simple: music as a personal and comedic resource in *Car Share*', in Liz Giuffre and Philip Hayward (eds), *Music in Comedy Television*, London: Routledge, pp. 170–85.

Moore, Charlotte (2019), 'A new vision for iPlayer, a new future for BBC television, bbc.co.uk, 7 October, <https://www.bbc.co.uk/mediacentre/speeches/2019/charlotte-moore-iplayer> (last accessed 20 August 2020).

Moran, Joe (2009), *On Roads*, London: Profile Books.

Morley, David (2010), 'Television as a means of transport: digital technologies and transmodal systems', in Jostein Gripsrud (ed.), *Relocating Television*, London: Routledge, pp. 257–70.

Morris, Nigel (2015), '"Do you like taster menus? Beyond hybridity: *The Trip* and *The Trip to Italy*', *New Review of Film and Television* 13.4: 422–42.

Morse, Margaret (1990), 'An ontology of everyday distraction: the freeway, the mall, and television', in Patricia Mellencamp (ed.), *Logics of Television: Essays in Cultural Criticism*, Bloomington: Indiana University Press, pp. 193–221.

Newbould, Chris (2017), 'Three's enough says *Trip to Spain* director Michael Winterbottom', *The National*, 14 September, <https://www.thenational.ae/arts-culture/film/three-s-enough-says-trip-to-spain-director-michael-winterbottom-1.628480> (last accessed 21 July 2020).

O'Donnell, Molly C. and Anne H. Stevens (2020), *The Microgenre: A Quick Look at Small Culture*, New York: Bloomsbury.

Peacock, Steven (2006), 'In between Marion and Geoff', *Journal of British Cinema and Television* 3.1: 115–21.

Peters, Jane, Koen van Eijck and Janna Michael (2018), 'Secretly serious? Maintaining and crossing cultural boundaries in the karaoke bar through ironic consumption', *Cultural Sociology* 12.1: 58–74.

Plowman, Jon (2018), *How to Produce Comedy Bronze*, London: Blink Publishing.

Puijk, Roel (2015), 'Slow television: a successful innovation in public service broadcasting', *Nordicom Review* 36.1: 95–108.

Rea, Steven (2011), '*The Trip*: Two British pals on a jocular jaunt', *The Philadelphia Inquirer*, 17 June, p. 5.

Red Bee Media (2020), 'Audiences in lockdown: how Covid-19 has supercharged the power of TV', 20 May, <https://www.redbeecreative.com/insights/blog/audiences-in-lockdown-how-covid19-has-supercharged-the-power-of-tv> (last accessed 18 January 2021).

Redshaw, Sarah (2008), *In the Company of Cars*, Aldershot: Ashgate.

Robinson, M. J. (2017), *Television On Demand*, New York: Bloomsbury.

Roxby, Phillipa (2014), 'How does commuting affect wellbeing?' bbc.co.uk, 22 February, <http://www.bbc.co.uk/news/health-26190236> (last accessed 18 January 2021).

Rustin, Susanna (2020), 'Imagine an end to our long love affair with cars', *The Guardian* (Opinion), 9 May, p. 4.

Saperstein, Pat (2011), 'B.O. takes side "Trip"', *Daily Variety*, 25 August, p. 3.

Schwartz, Alexandra (2020), 'The functionally dysfunctional matriarchy of *Better Things*', *The New Yorker*, 13 April, <https://www.newyorker.com/magazine/2020/04/20/the-functionally-dysfunctional-matriarchy-of-better-things> (last accessed 20 August 2021).

Sheller, Mimi (2004), 'Automotive emotions: feeling the car', *Theory, Culture & Society* 21.4/5: 221–42.

Sherwin, Adam (2016), '*The Trip*: Steve Coogan and Rob Brydon take hit TV show to Sky', *The Independent*, 15 February, <https://www.independent.co.uk/arts-entertainment/tv/news/the-trip-steve-coogan-and-rob-brydon-take-hit-tv-show-to-sky-a6875416.html> (last accessed 21 July 2020).

Skeggs, Beverley and Helen Wood (2012), *Reacting to Reality Television*, London: Routledge.

Sims, David (2017), 'The Trip to Spain is pure comedy comfort food', The Atlantic, 15 August, <https://www.theatlantic.com/entertainment/archive/2017/08/trip-to-spain- review/535914/> (last accessed 20 March 2021).
Smith, Zadie (2020), *Intimations*, London: Penguin.
Sweney, Mark (2016), 'James Corden's surprise US success won on YouTube views not ratings', *The Guardian*, 26 August, <https://www.theguardian.com/tv-and-radio/2016/aug/26/james-cordens-surprise-us-success-won-on-youtube-views-not-ratings> (last accessed 30 October 2020).
Thrift, Nigel (2004), 'Driving in the city', *Theory, Culture & Society* 21.4/5: 41–59.
Tryon, Chuck (2013), *On-Demand Culture*, New Brunswick: Rutgers University Press.
Turner, Graeme (2019), 'We need to talk about "binge-viewing"', *Television and New Media*, published online, 26 September.
Tussey, Ethan (2018), *The Procrastination Economy*, New York: New York University Press.
Underwood, Adam (2015), 'The Trip as mourning comedy', *Senses of Cinema*, March, Issue 74, <http://sensesofcinema.com/2015/feature-articles/the-trip-as-mourning-comedy/> (last accessed 7 February 2021).
V&A (2020), 'Cars: accelerating the modern world', <https://www.vam.ac.uk/exhibitions/cars> (last accessed 9 March 2021).
Van Dijck, José (2013), *The Culture of Connectivity*, Oxford: Oxford University Press.
Van Dijck, José, Thomas Poell and Martijn de Waal (2018), *The Platform Society*, Oxford: Oxford University Press.
Walters, Ben (2005), *The Office*, London: British Film Institute.
Walters, James (2013), 'Better or differently: style and repetition in *The Trip*', in Jason Jacobs and Steven Peacock (eds), *Television Aesthetics and Style*, London: Bloomsbury, pp. 113–24.
Waterson, Jim (2019), 'Alan Partridge saves Steve Coogan from lengthy driving ban', *The Guardian*, 13 August, <https://www.theguardian.com/culture/2019/aug/13/alan-partridge-saves-steve-coogan-from-lengthy-driving-ban> (last accessed 21 July 2020).
Wheatley, Helen (2016), *Spectacular Television*, London: I. B. Tauris.

# Index

Adele, 64, 131n
Adlon, Pamela, 36–37
advertising, 5–6, 10, 30–1, 32, 49, 54, 87, 89, 104, 122, 129n, 132n
algorithms, 55, 62, 111
Allen, Michael, 33, 39, 128n
Allen, Shane, 85, 108
Allison, Deborah, 29
Amazon Prime Video, 4, 81, 110
*American Auto*, 123
Apple, 16, 53, 66, 73, 110, 128n
apps, 81, 110
Arnheim, Rudolph, 118
aspect ratios, 22, 128n
*The A-Team*, 8
automobility, 9, 10, 11, 18, 44, 74, 77, 87, 122, 124
  representation, 18, 49, 50, 119

Baby Cow Productions, 23, 26, 28
Baddiel, David, 58, 132n
BAFTA, 27, 70, 87, 91, 114
*Bangers and Cash*, 5, 115, 133n
Barton, Laura, 45
BBC, 3, 17, 20, 28, 29, 50, 54, 84, 85, 107–8
  BBC1, 1, 2, 14, 26, 85, 88, 105, 110, 112, 115, 127n
  BBC2, 20, 26, 87
  Comic Relief, 63, 70, 89
  iPlayer, 14, 17, 81, 84–5, 88, 106, 108–13, 114, 133n

*Better Things*, 13, 15, 36–7, 50
Bieber, Justin, 53, 67, 70, 131n
*The Big Bang Theory*, 13, 75–6, 132n
Bignell, Jonathan, 7, 12
Bijsterveld, Karen, 75
binge-watching, 55, 85, 114–15
Bissel, David, 120
BMW, 7
Bonner, Frances, 91, 113
branded content, 6, 30–1, 129n
*The Bridge*, 7, 31
*Britain's Worst Driver*, 12–13, 17, 20
broadcasting, 16, 26, 28, 50, 64–5, 80, 84, 115, 118
  public service, 51, 88, 107–8
Brydon, Rob, 23, 25–9, 41, 45, 50, 128n
  performance of, 27, 31–48, 50, 128n
Bull, Michael, 74–5, 76
*Bullseye*, 2, 33
*Butterfly Kiss*, 29–30

camerawork, 12, 13, 21, 31–3, 44, 104, 125
  aerial, 31–2, 49
  location shooting, 30, 41, 45, 49, 56–7, 93
Cardwell, Sarah, 22, 128n
*Carpool*, 53, 55–8, 59, 60, 81, 131n
Carpool Karaoke (as digital content), 13, 14, 16, 17, 18, 38, 53, 63–83, 87, 116, 121, 124, 128n
*Carpool Karaoke Arabia*, 73

Index   145

*Carpool Karaoke Italia*, 17, 73–4
*Carpool Karaoke: The Series*, 66, 73, 128n
Cars
  and feeling, 9, 10, 60–1, 99–105, 123, 124
  female independence, 6, 10, 15, 36–7, 50, 98–9, 123
  masculinity, 4, 15, 35–6, 42–3, 47, 50, 98–9, 124, 127n
  as feature of modern life, 8, 117–19, 120–1, 124
  as TV characters, 7, 8
  social life of, 2, 13, 15, 21, 40–1, 92–9, 112, 120
  software aesthetic, 6, 96, 120
  *see also* habitat of cars
*Cars*, 8
*Catastrophe*, 50
CBS, 63, 66, 67, 80, 87
celebrity, 18, 33, 50, 69, 77, 83, 116
  interview, 58, 66, 67–9
Chalaby, Jean K., 4
Channel 4, 85, 90
*Chop Cut Rebuild*, 5
Clarkson, Jeremy, 2, 4, 125, 127n
*A Cock and Bull Story*, 27
Coleman, Paul, 106, 132n
*Comedians in Cars Getting Coffee*, 12, 13, 53, 55, 56, 58–63, 77, 79, 81, 131n
comedy (TV), 14, 27, 28–9, 36, 83, 122
  box-sets, 17, 107, 109–10, 111, 115
  car-based, 12, 13, 18, 14–15, 113, 116
  stand-up, 62, 89, 132n
  *see also* sitcom
commuting, 14, 18, 53, 69, 75, 82, 83, 86, 88, 91–7, 102, 105, 107, 116
congestion, 10, 121, 127n
*Content*, 119
Coogan, Steve, 23, 24, 25–9, 45, 85, 128n, 129n
  performance of, 27, 31–48, 50, 128n
Corden, James, 38, 41, 63–74, 76, 77, 82, 85, 87, 131n
Coren Mitchell, Victoria, 123
*Coronation Street*, 85, 131n

Covid-19, 17, 88, 105–12, 117
Crackle, 59, 79
Craig, David, 71, 79
Creeber, Glen, 80, 82
Cunningham, Stuart, 71, 79
*Curb Your Enthusiasm*, 13, 26, 33, 51

*Dad V Girls*, 13, 71–2, 131n
dashcams, 12, 63, 71, 119
Dave, 55, 57
David, Larry, 33, 60, 129n
Dent, Grace, 114, 115
digital shorts, 12
Dijck, José van, 54
distribution, 14, 66, 73
Dobrik, David, 53
docusoap, 5, 12, 115
dogging, 94, 104, 125
Drake, Philip, 127n
drama (TV), 5, 9, 29, 113
driver
  as host, 15, 69–70, 76
  comportment of, 9, 24
  incredulity, 46, 95–6, 102, 104
driverless cars, 120, 123–4
driving, 9, 10
  behaviours, 10–11, 18, 42–3, 48, 75–9, 93–4, 122–3
  cultures, 10, 11, 18, 60, 74, 96, 132n
  Los Angeles, 36, 95, 121
  as online micro-genre, 52, 53, 54–63, 67, 79
  *see also* automobility
*Driving School*, 20, 21, 22
*The Dukes of Hazzard*, 1
DVD bonus features, 32, 45

Edensor, Tim, 74, 132n
Emmy awards, 58, 70, 80
environmental sustainability, 10, 11, 31, 35, 121–2; *see also* greenwashing
Evans, Elizabeth, 73
everyday, the, 60, 82, 83, 88, 90–1, 97, 102, 116; *see also* 'television, ordinary'

Facebook, 52, 71, 120
Fallon, Jimmy, 63, 66, 67
Fiat, 74, 88, 95, 97, 98
Fife Donaldson, Lucy, 8–9, 38, 103–4
Ford, 7, 8
Ford, Sam, 69
Formula 1, 2–3, 125
Fry, Stephen, 57, 127n

*Gavin and Stacey*, 13, 23, 41, 43, 50, 70
Gibson, Sian, 86, 90, 106, 132n
Google, 52, 54, 123, 124
GoPro devices, 12, 81; *see also* mobile cameras
*The Grand Tour*, 4
Green, Joshua, 69
greenwashing, 35, 121–2, 129n
Groening, Stephen, 118
*Grandstand*, 1, 2
*The Guardian*, 29, 34, 45, 122

habitat of cars, 8, 11, 15, 21, 37, 50, 76, 82, 91, 93, 99–105, 125
Hall, Tony, 112
Hammond, Richard, 4
Haynes, Richard, 3
Heritage, Stuart, 12
Hill, Annette, 115
Honda, 32, 60, 129n
*How it Feels to Be Run Over*, 119
Hurtigruten, 46, 130n

Iannucci, Armando, 24
*Inspector Morse*, 7
internet, 14, 16, 18, 52, 53, 57, 62, 81
I-Spy, 19
ITV, 1, 3

Jaguar, 7, 8
Jaye, Victoria, 109
Jenkins, Henry, 69
Johnson, Catherine, 16, 55, 81, 109, 110
Johnson, Derek, 16
Jones, Jeffrey P., 63

journeys, 11, 24, 30, 39, 41, 43, 46, 49, 103–4; *see also* commuting

Kamm, Juergen, 15, 113
Katz, Jack, 95
Kay, Peter, 85–6, 88, 89–91, 106, 114, 132n, 133n
Kelly, J. P., 109–10, 133n
Klinger, Barbara, 76
*Knight Rider*, 1, 6, 9

*The Late Late Show with James Corden*, 53, 64–6, 70–3, 128n, 131n
Laurier, Eric, 11, 40–1, 69, 97
Lawson, Mark, 105, 113
Leno, Jay, 58
Letterman, David, 59, 61
*Life on Mars*, 7
light entertainment, 2, 35, 133n
Llewellyn, Robert, 53, 55–8, 61, 63, 81, 131n
Lobato, Ramon, 55, 57
Lochlann Jain, Sarah, 35
Lopez, Jennifer, 70, 82
Lorimer, Hayden, 11, 40–1, 69, 97
*Lost in Transmission*, 5
Lumsden, Lucy, 129n

McCabe, Janet, 33, 39, 128n
McNutt, Myles, 66, 80
Madonna, 68, 76, 77
*Marion and Geoff*, 13, 20–3, 50
Mason, Jennifer, 99, 102
*MasterChef*, 26, 29
Marx, Nick, 62
*Max and Paddy's Road to Nowhere*, 89, 132–3n, 134n
May, James, 4
Medhurst, Andy, 90
merchandise, 7–8, 131n
Miller, James, 118–19, 120
Mills, Brett, 21, 29, 41, 88, 95, 98, 100, 102–3, 125, 128n
Mini Cooper, 8, 38, 42, 50
mobile cameras, 12, 56, 63, 81, 119, 125

mobility, 9, 14, 69, 121, 124
  within audiovisual culture, 15, 62, 74, 82
  studies, 118–19, 125
*Modern Family*, 44, 50, 130n
Moran, Joe, 9, 88, 90, 98, 116
Morley, David, 118
Morse, Margaret, 118
Mortimer, Bob, 6, 47, 130n
*Mortimer & Whitehouse: Gone Fishing*, 47–8
*Motherland*, 50
motoring shows, 4, 5; *see also Top Gear*
motorsport, 1, 2–3
motorway service stations, 30, 42, 90–1
*Mr Bean*, 8, 15
MrBeast, 53, 131n
*Mud, Sweat and Gears*, 5
museum exhibitions, 8, 117, 127n
music (in cars), 37, 38–9, 42; *see also* singing
music video, 68, 101
*My Mother the Car*, 15

NASCAR, 3
naturalism, 15, 21, 49, 58, 91, 94, 100, 114, 125
Netflix, 16, 52, 53, 54–5, 62, 81, 84, 110, 112, 114
Neumann, Birgit, 15, 113
nostalgia, 7–8, 90, 102, 106, 112
Nyman, Michael, 39

Obama, Barack, 79
Obama, Michelle, 77–9, 131n
O'Donnell, Molly, 53
*The Office*, 86–7, 91, 92, 94
*One Foot in the Grave*, 95–6
online
  television, 52, 55, 80–1
  video, 12, 80
  *see also* YouTube
*Only Fools and Horses*, 7
*Outnumbered*, 44, 50

paratexts, 6, 31, 73
Partridge, Alan, 24
  *Alan Partridge: Alpha Pappa*, 24
  *I'm Alan Partridge*, 13, 24
passengering, 2, 13, 25, 40–8, 53, 73, 77, 87, 103
  conversation, 11, 12, 41–2, 44, 45, 48, 49, 56, 58, 93–9, 130n
  gendering, 15–16, 36, 42–3, 97–9
  proximity, 17, 107, 108
  sociology of, 11, 18, 39, 69, 122, 126
  *see also* singing
Payne, Alexander, 51
Payne, Candace, 72
*Peter Kay's Britain's Got the Pop Factor*, 86, 89
*Peter Kay's Car Share*, 12, 13, 14, 16–17, 18, 53, 84–116, 121, 124, 133n, 134n
platforms, 16, 51, 52–63, 66, 67, 80, 81, 107–12, 120, 124
Plowman, Jon, 27
*Police Camera Action!*, 119
police series, 7
*Police Squad!*, 15
Porsche, 7, 31
*The Price is Right*, 1
Puijk, Roel, 130n

Quibi, 79, 132n

radio, 75, 87, 91, 98, 99–105, 119, 123
*Radio Times*, 113
Rallycross, 1, 2, 3
Range Rover, 31, 32, 34–5, 48, 67, 74, 83, 87, 96, 129n
ratings, 65–6, 67, 113
realism, 31, 45
Red Bee Media, 108, 111
Redshaw, Sarah, 10
Reid, Tim, 132n
Reliant Regal, 7, 8
Renault, 6
Rimmer, Mark, 98, 100, 102–3

road, 17
 accidents, 98
 anthropology, 9, 18, 83, 88–9, 90–3
 trips, 13, 51, 127n
*Roary the Racing Car*, 8, 132n
Robeers, Timothy, 3
Robinson, M. J., 16
*The Royle Family*, 86–7, 91

sat-nav, 41, 96, 128n
Schwartz, Alexandra, 36
Seinfeld, Jerry, 56, 58–62, 79, 81, 130n
The Services (*Comedy Lab* episode), 90–1
Sheller, Mimi, 9, 10, 22, 61
*Sideways*, 51
singing, 32, 67–9, 74–9, 80, 82, 102–3, 125
sitcom, 12, 15, 18, 23, 27, 29, 41, 43, 44, 46, 49, 50, 55, 56, 84–8, 94, 98, 113–14, 123, 125
Skeggs, Beverley, 115
Sky, 28, 30, 51, 73, 129n
small screen
 aesthetics, 3, 12, 80–1, 82, 123
 intimacy, 22, 69, 71–2, 77, 80–2, 111–12, 125
smartphones, 16, 57, 58, 81, 82, 116, 118, 120
Smith, Angela, 127n
Smith, Zadie, 106, 117
social media, 13, 14, 53, 67, 70–3; 79, 80; *see also* vlogging
*The Sopranos*, 9
space of cars, 8, 9, 12, 18, 22–3, 38, 40–1, 44, 48, 58, 69, 71, 99, 103–4, 125
 as sonic world, 74–9, 96, 99–105
 *see also* aspect ratios
sports utility vehicle (SUV), 33–7, 50, 53, 68, 70, 74, 77, 79, 83, 87, 122, 129n
*Starsky and Hutch*, 1, 8, 127n
Stevens, Anne, 53
Stewart, Rod, 67, 77
Subaru, 122

talk shows, 12, 14, 53, 63–7, 131n
*Taxi*, 7
television
 genres, 3, 4, 13, 14
 industry, 5, 16, 17, 28, 87, 124
 medium of, 51, 65
 ordinary, 88, 91–2, 113, 115, 124
 performance, 8, 27, 33, 45, 103–4
 production, 2–3, 12, 61, 129n
 promos, 5, 6, 7, 30–1, 84
 slow, 46–8, 49
 spectacle, 3, 32
 sponsorship, 2, 5, 30–1, 60
 *see also* advertising
Television Studies, 4–5, 14, 65, 113, 114, 115, 118
Tesla, 124
*That Peter Kay Thing*, 89, 90, 134n
Thomas, Julian, 57
Thrift, Nigel, 96
TikTok, 73
title sequences, 6, 9, 59, 60
*The Tonight Show with Jimmy Fallon*, 64, 66, 131n
*Top Gear*, 3–5, 20, 24, 26, 29, 34, 50, 127n, 129n, 130n
Toyota (Prius), 33, 57, 129n
*Traffic Cops*, 5
trailers, 7, 66
transport policy, 10, 11, 121
*The Trip* series, 13, 14, 16–17, 18, 23–51, 59, 67, 82, 85, 87, 104, 122
 as films, 26, 128–9n
 *The Trip*, 25, 27, 29, 31, 32, 34, 38–9, 45, 83, 116
 *The Trip to Greece*, 26, 28, 34, 35, 43, 48, 122, 129n
 *The Trip to Italy*, 25, 33, 38, 41–2, 87
 *The Trip to Spain*, 26, 27–8, 30, 32, 38, 51, 53, 116, 129n, 131n
Turner, Graeme, 114, 115
Tussey, Ethan, 14, 81–2
Twitter, 70, 71, 133n
*230 Miles of Love*, 128n

video-on-demand, 16, 55, 59, 107–12
vlogging, 13, 14, 53–4, 63, 71–3, 125
Volkswagen, 5, 10, 60
Volvo, 30–1, 129n

*Wacky Races*, 6
Walters, James, 8–9, 38, 43–4, 47, 103–4
Wheatley, Helen, 32, 49
Whitehouse, Paul, 47, 130n
Wilson, Quentin, 20

Winston, Ben, 65, 66, 69, 70
Winterbottom, Michael, 26, 29–30, 31, 39, 45, 51, 128–9n
*Women Talking About Cars*, 123
Wonder, Stevie, 67–8, 70, 78, 82
Wood, Helen, 115

YouTube, 13, 14, 16, 53, 54, 55, 57, 64, 68–9, 70–1, 73, 80, 81, 87, 116, 131n
    channels, 56, 64, 65, 66, 120

CPSIA information can be obtained
at www.ICGtesting.com
Printed in the USA
JSHW030513170422
24885JS00013B/16